Fired Up! is packed with ideas, tips and practical information to help transform your business and accelerate performance. I have worked with Greg first hand and I know his book and his methods will improve your organization, get your staff motivated and achieve the goals you desire.

David Cooper
President, Premier Platforms

Fired Up! is a must-read for any leader who wants to accelerate their organization to achieve dynamic, bottom-line results. Chocked full of practical ideas, strategies and real-world examples, this book is a valuable asset to every leader in any industry.

Kathleen Occhiogrosso
Vice President of Human Resources/
CHRO Seton Health

Every person who wants to be an effective leader will benefit from Fired Up! Easy to read. Awesome material. A book you will not be able to put down.

John Tschohl
President, Service Quality Institute and author of
Achieving Excellence Through Customer Service

The only competitive edge businesses have today is the natural talent, ideas and suggestions of the workforce. Greg has compiled an excellent book that will help you and your organization become more innovative, engage your employees, and accelerate their performance. Every manager and business owner will benefit from this book; make it a reading requirement for your staff and keep a copy in the library.

Paula Davis
Executive Director, Employee Involvement Association

Greg Smith has hit a leadership homerun with Fired Up! If you are a seasoned professional, this book will refresh the leadership imperatives you learned along your career journey. If you are an emerging leader Fired Up! will provide invaluable insights on what it takes to move your organization and its people to the next level of excellence.

George V. Masi, FACHE
Executive Vice President & COO
Harris County Hospital District

Greg has done his homework in writing Fired Up! It is a "how to succeed" manual for leaders in any type of business. Fired Up will provide an organization's top leadership, managers and supervisors with proven ideas and strategies to lead, manage, communicate and motivate their most important asset, its people. His common sense message is very succinct, relevant and timely given the challenges of today's work environment. It is a must read for organizations seeking long term success.

Bill Schult Sr.
President, Maximum Potential Inc.

If you recruit, hire and manage people this book is a must read. It is jam-packed with proven concepts, smart business practices and easy-to-implement tips and techniques to help strengthen and transform every supervisor and manager in to the leader they have wanted to become. Great book!

Mel Kleiman, CSP
President, Humetrics

Fired Up!
Leading Your Organization
to Achieve Exceptional Results

ALSO BY GREG SMITH

The New Leader: Bringing Creativity
and Innovation to the Workplace

Tips 'N Techniques:
Dynamic Ideas to Reward, Energize
and Motivate Your Teams

Here Today, Here Tomorrow:
Transforming Your Workforce from
High-Turnover to High-Retention

Supervisor's Passport to Success:
A Quick and Easy Reference Guide for Managing People

Icebreakers and Teambuilding Exercises

401 Proven Ways to Retain Your Best Employees

Fired Up!

Leading Your Organization to Achieve Exceptional Results

GREGORY P. SMITH

Chart Your Course Publications
2814 Highway 212 SW
Conyers, Georgia, 30094
770-860-9464
www.ChartCourse.com

CHART
YOUR
COURSE
INTERNATIONAL

Chart Your Course Publications
2814 Highway 212 SW
Conyers, Georgia 30094

For a list of other publications or for more information, please call (800)
821-2487. In Alaska, Hawaii and internationally please call (770) 860-
9464 or visit http://www.ChartCourse.com
Smith, Gregory P.
Fired Up!
Leading Your Organization to Achieve Exceptional Results
246 pages:
ISBN: 978-0-9676843-6-9
Book Design by   BookDesign.ca
Printed in the United States of America

This book is dedicated to all those exceptional people who work on the front line everyday. If it were not for them, nothing would ever get accomplished.

I also dedicate this book to Jan King who inspires all of us and helps make Chart Your Course International a great place to work.

Contents

The Transformational Leader

Accelerate and Energize Breakthrough Performance

Creating a Great Place to Work

The Essentials of Great Customer Service

Manage for Top Performance

Turn Over a New Leaf — Avoid High Turnover

FIRED UP!

Author's Note

This book is a compilation of articles that were published between 2003 and 2010 in newspapers, the Navigator Newsletter and on Web sites around the world. While the business environment has certainly shifted in recent years and some of the companies referenced here may have changed ownership since the articles were first published, I believe the concepts these organizations employed remain relevant now more than ever. The reason is these companies placed a premium on encouraging their employees to learn about, participate in, and in many cases, even improve the corporate culture.

As the country works its way through this deep recession and prepares for a generation of workers to retire—or to not retire and choose to stay in the workforce longer, creating an impact on middle-aged workers—it will be more and more critical for businesses to motivate their employees, helping them develop loyalty and a sense of ownership in the companies where they choose to create careers.

On another matter, readers will note I have employed masculine pronouns in references made to individuals. I have chosen to do this as a point of style and ease only and I trust the readers will understand these scenarios apply equally to men and women alike.

Introduction

"Fired Up" is a book designed to help business owners, leaders and managers build a high energy work culture that accelerates individual and organizational performance. As a result, you will create a great place to work that makes more money, generates higher sales and provides outstanding service to your customers and workers alike.

It is clear, as evidenced through the numerous examples in this book of successful strategies employed by these organizations, that money is not the primary motivator of workers.

The truth is people want to contribute to their companies in their own way. The challenge for leaders and managers is to discover how to tap into those talents and create a positive culture at work. This is especially true today when morale in the workplace is lower than ever before. A 2010 survey conducted by the Conference Board showed only 45 percent of Americans are satisfied with their work. This is the lowest level ever recorded by the Conference Board in more than 22 years of research. Those that fail to improve job satisfaction are at risk of losing their top talented people to the competition.

Sadly, many workers have been mismanaged and inculcated in an environment where employees are trained that they should be grateful they have a job at all, squelching any motivation and freedom to look for better ways to do things. As a consequence, workers become more and more disengaged with their jobs.

The resulting repercussions will be that, as the economy improves and the job market widens, people will flee their current jobs, jumping like rats off a sinking ship. Weak or struggling companies will falter through the loss of experienced employees, and fall further behind than they are now.

The harsh reality is these companies will ultimately spend more money and resources to hire and train talented and committed people than if they had invested in the ones they already have.

So, what's the antidote for this corporate malaise? People need to get fired up—and that's the responsibility of leaders. Leaders and managers have to get out from behind their desks and get on the front lines. This will not only inspire and motivate your employees, but it will transform your organization to achieve amazing results. "Fired Up!" is a useful tool along this road.

—Greg

I

The Transformational Leader

1.

Traits of Fired-Up Leaders

Leaders do not become leaders because of an election, a title or because it's written in a job description. Some believe people are born natural leaders. Some people believe managers are leaders by virtue of being managers. Both these statements are far from the truth. People become leaders only when others accept them as leaders. The title "leader" is bestowed upon an individual and it something that must be earned. While some leaders seem to have a charismatic talent, most people become good leaders by trial and error.

There are eight key traits fired-up leaders share:

1. Leaders have a clear mission.

Good leaders have a defining mission in their life. This mission can be called many things: a purpose, an obsession or a calling. Its name is unimportant, but what is important is that this mission, above all other traits, separates titular managers from true leaders. The movie *Saving Private Ryan* clearly demonstrated this point. Captain John Miller (Tom Hanks) was able to unite his men and create purpose in their horrific mission to find and rescue Private James Ryan. iuyiuy

2. Leaders create big ideas.

Good leaders have big ideas and dare others to be great. Billy Payne ignited a vision in the hearts and minds of the people of Georgia and the world. His vision caught fire and brought the Centennial Olympic Games to Atlanta in 1996. Despite many naysayers' criticisms, it was one of the best Games ever. When the Summer Olympics ended that year, Billy Payne said, "I am a nondescript, regular old person who had an idea."

3. Leaders trust their people.

An effective leader is not a micromanager. Responsibility is pushed down through the ranks in order to rely on the ideas and energies of the entire workforce. This delegation of authority requires that employees have a voice in the decision-making process, which magnifies the leader's ability to effectively lead others.

4. Leaders remain calm in a crisis.

Leaders take a position and defend it when things go awry. Being graceful and brave under fire is the surest way to build credibility.

5. Leaders encourage innovation.

If an organization does not examine new ways of doing things, if it does not push out its boundaries or never makes mistakes, it increases its chances of becoming obsolete. Herbert Kelleher, former CEO of Southwest Airlines, has a nonconformist leadership philosophy. Kelleher believes everyone is a leader and he empowers people to make decisions. To fight bureaucratic rules and regulations, he pushes decision-making authority to the lowest possible level. As Kelleher says, "We tell our people that we value inconsistency."

6. Leaders are experts.

Good leaders are intimately familiar with their organization's products and services. Nothing replaces experience on the front line. All executives, managers and supervisors should spend time on the front line to find out what is happening and prevent what keeps their workforce from doing their best. Again, it is a question of establishing credibility. People soon know when a superior is "winging it" and that's when they stop listening.

7. Leaders know what is essential.

Leaders have a remarkable ability to zero in on what is important. They can simplify complex problems elegantly without taking the easy way out.

8. Leaders teach and mentor others.

In this rapidly changing environment, organizations must create a culture of learning. The senior people must be teaching and training those who may soon replace them. This does not necessarily mean conducting formal classroom training. Instead, leaders should be talking to people in the hallway, on the loading dock . . . everywhere. Everyone should be mentoring someone.

Whether you call yourself CEO, president, leader, manager, elected official, religious leader or supervisor, we are expected to set the example for others. The needs of those we lead should come before OUR needs.

2

Become a Better Leader by Showing People You Care

I once overheard a conversation between two co-workers. One of the women said, "He's a nice guy. He makes me feel good about working here."

This young lady was talking about her new boss. Like many employees, she was more influenced by her employer's "soft" skills than his technical skills. His interpersonal skills were what mattered most—his ability to communicate, motivate and show genuine concern. These soft skills are an important aspect of creating a good place to work. When a manager lacks these skills, or actively cultivates their hard-edged opposites, workers who have choices will jump ship.

When an employee leaves, he hasn't quit the company -- he quit his boss. Chart Your Course International completed a survey that showed half the people quit their previous employer because of their first-line supervisor. That's a painful statistic when you consider how difficult it is to find good people. This is also sad when you look at the bottom line and it's foolish when you do nothing about.

Managers today have a difficult job. It is not easy. The responsibilities and demands are immense. People expect more and some are just plain difficult to work with. It should go without saying those businesses that do a good job selecting, training and developing their managers will enjoy higher productivity and lower turnover. The two go hand in hand.

Soft skills reign supreme and are critical for success. Unfortunately, most businesses do a miserable job selecting and training their managers. Many management development programs focus entirely on the technical aspects of the job and not people skills. Some managers are tyrants and make life miserable for those they are supposed to lead. It is people skills that make the difference.

I joined the Army after I graduated from college. My first boss was an exceptional leader. He was a combat veteran and a former Special Forces medic in Vietnam. He was the type of person who always put the needs of others before his own interests. He would not ask you to do something he would not do himself.

As one of the junior officers in my company, I had the odious responsibility of having to "pull duty." Pulling duty consisted of working a 24-hour shift. As luck would have it, my shift fell on New Year's Eve – the worst day of the year to have duty. It was considered the worst day because the young soldiers I was in charge of were partying and getting into general mischief all night long. They did all the things young soldiers typically do on New Year's Eve.

The next morning did not arrive soon enough. I was a victim of a long, sleepless night and could not wait to get home. It was early Saturday morning and I still had several hours to go before I could leave. The phone rang. It was Joe, my boss. He wanted to know if I had made any plans for lunch. He informed me that he and his wife had prepared something for me to eat and wanted to know if it was OK to bring it over. I want you to know I don't remember what the food was, but it was a meal I will never forget.

That one small act of kindness showed me he really cared. That one small act taught me more about leadership than all the degrees and diplomas hanging on my wall. There is an old saying in the military: "If you take care of your troops, your troops will take care of you." The point is, management is an eight-to-five obligation, but true leadership is a 24-hour-a-day responsibility.

Here are a few suggestions to consider in your management development process:

- Have executives share their goals and expectations;
- Allow employees to evaluate their supervisors using a 360-degree evaluation;
- Hold managers accountable and responsible for retention;
- Provide the support and training to help managers do their jobs;
- Start measuring the financial cost of turnover and apply the cost to the bottom line;
- Conduct exit interviews to discover the true reasons people quit;

- Train managers how to become good leaders;
- Reward managers for positive retention and productivity; and
- Conduct an internal climate assessment at least twice a year.

3

What Good Leaders Do

What is the difference between a manager and a leader? Answer: EVERYTHING. Many organizations suffer from a lack of leadership. Leadership is the art and science of influencing others to achieve goals by providing purpose, direction and motivation. A leader is a person who inspires you to take a journey to a destination you wouldn't go to by yourself.

Leadership spans a narrow gap between two key areas: passion for action and passion for people. A bold orientation for action matched with compassion for people creates an emotional energy transforming the ordinary into the extraordinary.

Retired General William Livsey said, "You can assign a man to a leadership position, but no one will ever really be a leader until his appointment is ratified in the hearts and minds of his soldiers." Leadership is earned. It is not based on titles, position or rank. The business that neglects its people and treats them solely as expendable resources stands to incur the greatest loss. A people-oriented leader understands how, why and what motivates people at work.

Far too many organizations have a bottom-line, short-term, mentality. Productivity largely has to do with a softer side of management. Bob Moawab, CEO of the Edge Learning Institute says, "Most organizations help people become better employees. The best organizations help employees become better people."

Change in the business environment was at one time orderly and incremental. In an orderly business environment, managers do well. However, change is much more dramatic now. Famed economist and management consultant Peter Drucker puts it bluntly by saying, "Every organization has to prepare for the abandonment of everything it does." These factors require leadership—the ability to lead, not manage.

A manager maintains status quo. A leader charts a course and looks over the horizon. Rapid changes in technology, an uncertain economy, competition, regulatory requirements and an increasingly diverse workforce are factors forcing organizations to adapt quickly to new circumstances.

4
The Myths of Leadership

Joel Barker, a scholar and an expert on paradigm shifts in the corporate world, provides one of the best definitions of leadership. He said, "A leader is someone you would follow to a place you would not go to by yourself." Leadership is about getting things done and helping individuals and organizations reach their potential. My experience shows most organizations do a pitiful job helping people reach their potential. One reason for this is old-fashioned leadership techniques—out-dated leadership concepts or what I call, "leadership mythology."

I am amused when someone tells me they have to check with their "leadership team" before they can make a decision. When I hear this, I know this organization is in trouble. Leadership is not a team, a job title or a position of authority. Leadership is what a person does. A leader is someone who will challenge the status quo.

A myth is a fallacy that is believed to be true. As in many things in life, there are myths surrounding the concept and practice of leadership. Unfortunately, these myths sometimes prevent people from reaching their full potential as leaders.

By listing these leadership myths, it is my hope to dispel many of the false beliefs.

Myth 1 - Leadership is a rare ability only given to a few.
Many people think a leader is born not made. This can't be further from the truth. Most people have the potential to become good leaders, but leadership is not like a diet pill. Like most learned skills, it takes time, training and a tremendous amount of trial and error. The key ingredient that makes people good leaders is the ability to care about others. The second ingredient is a sense of purpose, vision or mission. A good leader charts a course and provides direction to those they lead.

Myth 2 - Leaders are charismatic.
Some of the world's most famous leaders had warts—some sort of shortcoming or personality limitation. In a leadership role, people skills are important, maybe even more important than technical skills. However, the best leaders are those who work toward a goal. Your cause, your purpose and your mission in life will make you charismatic, not the other way around.

Myth 3 - The person with the title or highest rank or position is the leader.
Ideally, the senior person in the business should be a good leader. However, authentic leadership is not based on position or rank. It is based on action, performance, ability and effectiveness. We all relate to working for those people placed in leadership roles who did more to demoralize and destroy the business than anything else.

The best companies strive to develop and create as many leaders as possible. W.L. Gore & Associates, makers of Gore-Tex and other products, has a unique approach to leadership. The company practices natural leadership, "leadership by followship." They don't appoint or promote people as their leaders; they let the authentic leaders surface to the top. People gravitate to those they want to follow and work alongside. W.L Gore & Associates does not have job descriptions, job titles and only a few rules and regulations. If a person comes up with a new product idea, he puts together a team of people who have the desire and knowledge to make it work.

Myth 4 - Effective leadership is based on control, coercion and manipulation.

Leadership is about the future, not the past. Remember Joel Barker's quote about leadership: "A leader is someone you would follow to a place you would not go to by yourself." Good leaders gain followers out of respect and their ability to get people to work toward a particular goal or achieve a destination. People follow because they can relate to the vision or goal personalized by the leader. A good leader helps people become better than they are. A good leader creates a work environment that attracts, keeps and motivates its workforce.

Myth 5 - Good leaders have more education than other people.

Educational degrees may mean you have a good education, but they don't necessarily mean you are a good leader. When it comes to leadership, experience is the best teacher. The U.S. military has the best leadership development program in the world. In the military, you start out at the bottom. You are placed in leadership positions and evaluated closely. As your experience broadens, so does your responsibility. This practical experience is reinforced with weeks and months of formal training throughout the individual's career.

The secret of success is those years of experience on the front line. This is where a person learns to manage those interactions, experiences and conflicts. They learn how to balance the needs of the mission versus the needs of the individual. Those officers and non-commissioned officers who fail to advance must exit the military. The military model of leadership development may not be perfect, but it remains unequalled by any other organization.

5

The Sinking of the Titanic Provides Lessons for Leaders

"We have struck iceberg ... sinking fast ... come to our assistance." On a cold evening in 1912 that message came blistering across the airwaves. Before they tapped the last bit of Morse code, those words became the epitaph over the lives of the 1,200 people lost on the Titanic. The ship was doomed as it slowly sank into its watery grave. Why did the largest, most-advanced ship of the time sink?

Those of us who study history or remember the movie may know why. It wasn't the iceberg that caused the disaster, but something else. Clear in my mind was the real cause: failed leadership.

Leadership is Always Responsible

Leadership is responsible for everything the organization does or fails to do. Leadership is more than a wooden figurehead. A leader is not a position, job title, or in this case, the captain of the ship. Leadership is not about power, ego or pride. Leadership is ever-present, touching, motivating, talking, checking and removing barriers, training, preparing, breathing and moving about.

The Titanic's ill-fated voyage was Captain E.J. Smith's retirement trip. He was headed for the easy life. All he had to do was get to New York. God only knows why he ignored the facts, why he disregarded seven iceberg warnings from his crew and other ships.

The Titanic still rests on the bottom of the ocean, but we can resurrect the truth and apply a few lessons learned to help us become better leaders.

The Biggest Is Not the Best

Today's businesses must change course quickly. It took over 30 seconds before the Titanic turned away from the iceberg, but by then it was too late. The larger an organization becomes, the greater its inflexibility. The more difficult and cumbersome it is to steer, to direct and to change course. Large businesses soon grow into huge bureaucracies where rules, regulations, policies, procedures and "I need permission to make a decision" become the norm.

Rank Has Its Privileges?

Ranking is good for command and control, but not good for change and innovation. Ranking people limits their potential. Today, businesses rank and classify people—sometimes unintentionally. Whether it is reserved parking spaces for the privileged or being categorized as blue collar, white collar, temporary, part-time, those with cubicles or those with offices, the results are the same. Clear the lines between the classes and make everyone feel they are rowing in the same direction, for the same purpose. In a disaster, everyone is equal.

The Truth Changes

The Titanic was unsinkable, so they thought. The ship designers were so confident in their ship they only had enough lifeboats for half the passengers. The thinking that made us successful yesterday will cause us to fail tomorrow. Our unlearning curve must be greater than our learning curve if we are going to succeed.

Advanced Technology Makes a Poor Substitute for Bad Leadership

When technology fails, leadership must prevail. Captain Smith said years before the Titanic's voyage, "I cannot imagine any condition which would cause a ship to founder. Modern shipbuilding has gone beyond that." Many businesses today have placed the wrong people in charge. They are not leaders, but managers. So when disaster strikes, who is going to step up and lead, or will your technology pull you under?

Leadership is About Training and Development

As the stern of the Titanic lifted out of the water, the crew and passengers struggled with the lifeboats. There had been no drills, no rehearsals, and the crew stood unfamiliar with their responsibilities. The boats were improperly loaded and only one went back to try to recover survivors. A good leader helps people improve their skills so they can become more productive.

What Lies Below Is More Destructive than What Is On Top

The greatest dangers lie unseen below the surface. That night in 1912 the water was smooth like glass—deceptively dangerous. The iceberg lurked below. Like steel fangs, it tore at the rivets along 300 feet of the Titanic's hull. Those below, the crew and steerage, felt and saw the damage first. Like a gasping breath, the steam billowed above as chaos reigned below. Then and now, those who know what's wrong with your "ship" are those below decks. Those people on the frontline usually have the best ideas and solutions to your problems. Consider asking them for their ideas and suggestions before catastrophe strikes.

Leadership Looks Beyond the Horizon

A good "Captain" is on the lookout for shifting trends, changing needs, storms and icebergs. Wal-Mart founder Sam Walton identified and met a need while other retailers did not. Apple saw the need for the iPod while others were still happy with CD players. The vision of the Sony Walkman existed in Akio Morita's mind well before it entered the mind of the competition. Get the picture? Be on the lookout, scanning the horizon for the next wave of change instead of waiting for it to hit you in the face.

6

Building Your Trust and Credibility Factor

Building trust and credibility as a leader is like building a house. It begins with a plan, laying a solid foundation and proceeding one step at a time. Whether this is your first supervisory position or you are an experienced manager, you should progress with your transition methodically the first 90 days on the job. How do you quickly establish yourself with those you lead? What do you do first? Here are a few ideas to consider:

Get the facts before making major decisions.
Don't allow yourself to be pressured in making major changes or big decisions during the beginning of your transition. Try to take a low-key approach until you are ready for your first meeting with your team. Gather information, see how things are done and get to know your people before disrupting status quo. Once you gain "acceptance," understand why they do what they do, then your people will more willingly support you, your changes and your leadership style.

Identify the informal leaders.

Informal leaders will make you or break you. The first thing I did when taking over a new assignment was to find and try to befriend the informal leaders. Informal leaders are those who control and influence people in your office or organization. In the beginning they have more power than you do. In some situations, the informal leader has more credibility and is held in higher respect than the formal leader. But sometimes they are irritants. Nonetheless, try to make them your allies so they don't sabotage what you are trying to do. If you work in a unionized environment, make sure you keep union officials informed and involved as much as possible.

Find the history.

Discover what successes your group is proud of. A leader gains respect when he takes the time to know what the group has done in the past. Recognizing accomplishments of the past will help build your credibility for future goal-setting.

Interview your people.

I worked for a leader who personally interviewed everyone in the organization. This is time consuming but it paid dividends. It took several weeks, but he immediately established himself, gained the respect of everyone and captured critical information. Since you are new and perceived as neutral, people are more willing to tell you the "truth" about the work environment. Here are some questions to ask:

- What can I do to help you accomplish your goals?
- What is keeping you from doing your best?
- What makes you feel appreciated?

- What did my predecessor do that we should continue?

- What did my predecessor do that we should stop?

- Are you considering leaving this job for another? Why?

- What do you see as my role in this organization?

- What direction do you think we should go?

Begin problem-solving.

With the information gained from the interviews, begin making changes to some of the common issues or problems affecting your group. This will show you are serious about helping make work life better.

Conduct a meeting.

Wait to have a meeting until you have something specific to say and enough background information to speak with authority. At the meeting highlight the employees' past successes, some of the issues or problems affecting the group and what you plan to do. Talk about some of the changes you are considering and why. Here are some other items to cover in this meeting:

- Your background and experience;

- Just enough personal information to show you are human;

- Your expectations;

- Your pet peeves;

- Your leadership style;

- How they should approach you with problems; and

- What to do with new ideas and suggestions.

Set goals and standards.

Now that you have gained the respect and trust of your group you are ready to set goals for the future. There are many ways to set goals, but the main thing is not to do it in the dark. If you followed these steps in this article, goal setting will be a piece of cake. Your style of leadership and experience will dictate the best way.

7

Become an Agent of Change

Change in the 21st century is like sailing a ship during a storm. Waves are coming at you from every direction. Hidden rocks threaten to tear your ship apart. The water never stops churning and there is no time to rest. Falling overboard is a scary possibility, and if you fail to work together to chart a course, disaster could very well be your companion.

Today's economic climate requires a sense of urgency. There are no guarantees tomorrow will bring the same success we experienced in the past. How can we survive in this type of environment? We need to become leaders and agents of change. People will learn to read the ocean, prepare for the storm, avoid the rocks, work as a team and feel the excitement of becoming a different, better organization.

"Change before you have to," says Jack Welch, former CEO of General Electric and one of the most quoted CEOs in the world today. He goes on to talk about "continuous improvement" (incremental and evolutionary change) and "transformation" (quantum and revolutionary change), urging companies to embrace both types as the only way to survive in today's global competitive environment.

Why is change so difficult for companies to initiate and for employees to accept? We resist even the best ideas because we are comfortable with the status quo. Changes often fail, and employees are sometimes adversely affected; therefore, change we perceive as negative is resisted or ignored. Many times executives fail to make those critical, gut-wrenching changes that could save or sink their companies. It is easy to keep doing what you have always done—even if it is wrong or obsolete. Many companies want to change but few execute it well.

Two basic types of change are reactive and proactive. Reactive change occurs after external forces (usually competition, customers or government) have already adversely affected performance. If you lose a major account or your product is suddenly obsolete, you have no choice. Something must be done to survive, and this type of change can be desperate and very stressful.

The other type of change is proactive. This is initiated to take advantage of some opportunity such as a new market or an opportunity for cost savings. Generally, proactive change is more deliberate and satisfying. A company justifying and purchasing a new piece of equipment or an expansion into a new office can be very exciting.

Resistance to change is natural. People have concerns about how it will affect their jobs and welfare. Employees also have uncertainty about whether or not the change will be in the organization's best interests or even if it will be around six months from now. Some say, "This is just another program that will be gone soon. We've tried things like this before."

And so the organization goes through the painful change process that involves shock, denial, suffering, resistance, acceptance, and finally commitment. Sometimes this process can take months or even years.

If change is inevitable and if Mr. Welch is right about actually proactively seeking ways to change, how can we do it better and less painfully? Here are some ways we may become better change agents and overcome resistance:

- Preparation and vigilance—Remember the Titanic? Never be satisfied with status quo. All businesses will eventually face the storm. The ones that survive will be the ones prepared.

- Education and communication—Although it takes time and effort, the very best approach is through letting people know as much as you can as soon as you can. People least resist what they know and understand. Start the process early and communicate the progress frequently.

- Participation and ownership—To the extent possible, let people help make the decisions and participate in making the change. When they are involved, it becomes "our" project rather than "their" project. When problems occur, they get solved more quickly and quietly. Support comes from involved people.

- Facilitation and support—New skills may be required to manage change and support the new way of doing things. Training overcomes insecurity. It is important for people to understand the change process and remove barriers to its success.

■ Strong leadership – Owners and managers must be committed and make their feelings known to subordinates. Sometimes leadership may involve communicating a strong message, and other times it may be to offer encouragement. If there is no leadership, there will be no commitment.

8

Top 10 Strategies for a High-Performance Organization

Fear and anxiety dominate the workplace. People are feeling depressed and scared. Those who have jobs are waiting anxiously for the other shoe to drop. Millions of people feel victimized by the economy. Others have given up hope. The effect is lowering motivation and job productivity the world over.

Well, it is a good thing I don't feel that way—I refuse to be a pessimist.

Whether you are the president of the United States or the president of the local PTA, you have a tremendous opportunity to make a difference in the lives of others through the words you use and the attitude you choose.

If you are a leader, you have a higher calling—a responsibility to set a positive example for others to follow. Now more than ever, this world, this country and your business need optimistic leadership. The people you influence are looking for hopefulness and a positive direction to follow. This is what good leaders provide.

In my own experiences I have learned time and time again with the right leadership, people can do amazing things. Let's pledge here and now to be more optimistic. If we do, we will snap out of this recession much quicker. Consider the following 10 strategies:

1) Create purpose and vision for the future.
The term "purpose" refers to the primary reason an organization exists. The primary role is to inspire and guide the setting of values. Purpose gives people a reason why they should work for this organization. The vision of the organization is known by all and shows where the organization is headed.

2) Deploy a leadership strategy.
There is unmistakable evidence revealing how leadership is exercised, formally and informally, throughout the organization. It is clear how key decisions are made, communicated and carried out. We have structures and systems for decision-making; selection and development of leaders and managers; and reinforcement of values, directions and performance expectations.

3) Provide direction and lead by example.
Leaders in the organization serve as role models through their ethical behavior and personal involvement in planning, communication and coaching, as well as their development of future leaders, organizational performance and employee recognition.

4) Be comfortable creating change.

Look at other innovations and industries to see beyond the horizon for new trends. The successful organization does not maintain status quo, but should make meaningful change to improve its programs, services, products and processes to create new value for the organization's stakeholders.

5) Tear down walls and barriers.

Dedicate time pinpointing and removing barriers, obstacles and non-essential work that obstruct workflow, communication and productivity. Insure individuals are free to go to anyone in the organization for advice and assistance. Conduct an employee satisfaction survey to pinpoint areas of dissatisfaction.

6) Create a charged environment that engages the workforce.

Success depends on valuing each employee's satisfaction, motivation, well-being and development. People have a basic human need to feel appreciated. Recognition programs help meet that need as well as generate behavior in alignment with organizational goals and standards.

7) Hire and retain top talent.

Retention begins by recruiting and hiring top performers. Implement a formal retention program and carefully consider what attracts, keeps and motivates the workforce. Place effort toward understanding and analyzing why people depart the organization. Create flexible work-life arrangements for your employees.

8) Manage ideas and innovation.

Create a system to learn and apply new knowledge, trends and ideas through evaluation, study, experience and innovation. Provide formal and informal training programs, improvement cycles and benchmarking. Capture ideas and suggestions from employees and staff to achieve this. Insure you embed these processes in the way the organization operates.

9) Customer and market focus.

One of the most important priorities should be a focus on the needs and expectations of customers. Do you build and maintain relationships with customers? Do you have metrics in place to measure customer satisfaction and loyalty? Add additional points if this information is shared with all of your staff/employees. Empower employees to satisfy customers on first contact, improve processes, and raise productivity to achieve business results.

10) Manage and measure performance.

Insure your organization has a numerical process that quantifies input, output, and measures all critical performance outcomes. Identify your critical processes and measure how these processes impact on organizational success.

9

Heroic Leadership – Crash Landing in the Hudson River

The heroic actions demonstrated by Captain Chesley "Sully" Sullenberger and his outstanding crew on US Airways Flight 1549 are worthy of admiration.

We have grown callous by all the negative images we see in the media. We are bombarded in our daily news with fallen titans motivated by corruption, ego and greed. Whether it concerns peanut butter, private jets or golden parachutes, we have grown skeptical and less trusting of those in authority. It is no surprise why so many people were mesmerized by this incident of a pilot who put others first.

First, we heard of the actual incident -- a perfectly executed crash landing in the Hudson River resulting in no loss of life. But the extraordinary happening is more remarkable when we examine it deeper.

If we dissect this event, each of us appreciates something different. Neither space nor time permits me to list every detail, but here are a couple that stand out most in my mind:

The passengers came first. Once the plane was in the water, "Sully" was the last to abandon ship. He did not get off until everyone was outside the plane. Captain Sullenberger has become an international celebrity, but you still sense his humility – he is not a man selfishly seeking glory.

We tend to forget there are far more good people in this world than bad. Sullenberger and his crew made us hopeful and proud again. That is a good thing.

10

Today's Businesses Need "Gladiator" Leaders

Remember the heart-pounding, soul-stirring message of the movie, "Gladiator"? Remember how Maximus, Russell Crowe's character, rallied his men around him and led them to victory, even in the face of almost certain defeat? Remember his "envision the goal" technique for getting through the horrors of battle? Now, consider the leadership in your own company. Are there any gladiators in the ranks? Are you a gladiator?

The time is right for a more heroic style of leadership. Desperate times lend themselves to the rise of gladiators. Instead of seeing today's economy as a negative, executives should view it as an opportunity in disguise—a chance to position your organization for the inevitable economic up-swing. Here are eight virtues of "gladiator" leadership:

1. Gladiators have a mission for which they feel real passion. Call it a purpose, an obsession, a calling; whatever the terminology, good leaders have a defining mission in their life. This mission, above all other traits, separates managers from leaders. In "Gladiator," Maximus lived for the

mission of killing the evil usurper Commodus and restoring Rome to the values that made her great.

2. Gladiators create a vision. Having and communicating a clear picture of a future goal will lead to its achievement. Dare to think great! Maximus helped his fellow gladiators see they could overthrow their enemies and survive the horror of the battles in which they were forced to participate. In business, a leader may create an "enemy"—the economy, the competition, inefficiency—to challenge the energies of his people and give them something to fight for.

3. Gladiators lead from the front—they don't dictate from the back. In the movie, when Maximus was a general and when he was a gladiator, he fought up front where the firestorm was heaviest. And so does a good business leader. Working "in the trenches" shows you're not afraid to get your hands dirty, it helps you fully understand the issues your "soldiers" are facing and inspires loyalty in your troops.

4. Gladiators know there is strength in teams. Where would Maximus have been if he hadn't trusted his men to fight with him and cover his back? Likewise, where would you be without your employees? While the gladiator leader has the skills to draw people together, he doesn't hog the spotlight. He has care and compassion for his team and wants every member to be recognized for his efforts. This is especially important in a time when the old style "command and control" structure is waning. Younger workers (those from Generations X and Y) tend to be loyal to their co-workers rather than the traditional "organization."

5. Gladiators encourage risk-taking. In the Roman Empire, gladiators were expected to die with honor. Refusing to lie down and let one's opponents win was bucking the status quo. And certainly killing the reigning emperor—however corrupt—simply was not done. If a company does not examine its way of doing things, if it does not push out its boundaries, if it never makes mistakes, it may become roadkill.

6. Gladiators keep their heads in a crisis. Maximus had to think on his feet and refuse to give into terror and panic. He faced the most formidable foes with calm and focus. Business leaders must do the same. They must take a position and defend it when things go awry. Being graceful and brave under fire is the surest way to build credibility— a necessity for sound leadership. Gladiators don't retreat due to the slowing economy, but look for the opportunity under their feet.

7. Gladiators prepare for battle 24 hours a day. A Roman gladiator was essentially a fighting machine. To stay alive, his mind had to be constantly on the upcoming battle. Business leaders, likewise, must be obsessed with training and developing their people in good times and bad. People need and want to hone their individual skills and to "sharpen their swords." Furthermore, good leaders must constantly learn what's necessary to survive and unlearn the "old rules." Just because a management style worked a decade ago does not mean it will work in today's economy; good leaders evolve with the times.

8. Gladiators are teachers and mentors. Maximus taught his men the lessons they would need to survive in their new

role as gladiators. In today's rapidly changing environment, leaders must also teach and train those who may soon replace them. This does not necessarily mean formal classroom training. We need leaders who are approachable and willing to talk to everyone in the organization. Everyone should be mentoring someone.

II

Accelerate and Energize
Breakthrough Performance

11

The Best Way to Predict the Future Is to Invent It

As part of my normal routine I read dozens of magazines, newspapers, books and reliable sources of information on the Internet. As a side note, the least dependable source of content is cable television news.

In the May 4, 2009 edition of Fortune Magazine, I enjoyed reading an article by Anne Mulcahy, the CEO of Xerox. I believe she hit the nail on the head regarding what business should be doing during this economic downturn.

She said, *"I know from experience one of the biggest mistakes that can be made right now is to slash investments in innovation. And by innovation, I don't just mean product research and development. It can also be innovating in new markets, launching new businesses, and even disruptive innovation in work processes."* Then she added, *"I remind my team that the next generation of technology and services will be born out of decisions we make at this unique moment in time. With that, we're banking on the advice of Alan Kay, a former Xerox researcher, who said, 'The best way to predict the future is to invent it."*

I have had an interesting seat watching business after business cut back, terminate talented people, eliminate training and development, and curtail important projects. Instead of taking a proactive approach, these businesses are just creeping along the highway hoping they don't become the next roadkill. Many have laid off their most experienced people, virtually wiping out their talent pool and future leadership.

Yes, survival is paramount and businesses have had to make difficult decisions. However, by making the wrong choices, many of these businesses have only put a noose around their necks. They have placed themselves in a precarious position, unprepared when the economy starts improving.

Studies show layoffs end up being far more costly and damaging than the short-term money they end up saving. As Anne Mulcahy states in her article, businesses can't stop innovating. Take for example that some companies have cut back on customer service. So instead of increasing customer loyalty, they have only alienated their customers. In my book, that is the kiss of death. If you work in that kind of place, you might as well box up your stuff because it won't be long until the business collapses and you're the next out the door.

The turbulent economy has placed businesses and business leaders under pressure to improve and restructure their organizations. A survey by The Conference Board showed executives' major concern was about "speed, flexibility and adaptability to change." Businesses need to implement a transformational style of leadership along with an effective strategy that will enhance productivity and position their business or organization for increased efficiency.

I spoke at a meeting held by the Economic Development Council in Longview, Texas. This community of 80,000 people is focused on a bright future. Despite the economy, they are still growing and remain dynamic interested to learn new techniques to keep their employees motivated and working effectively.

Several of the people who attended my session work at the Neiman Marcus distribution center. They are responsible for distributing merchandise to stores all across the U.S. It was encouraging to me to see this organization still cares for its people and wants to stay vital, innovative and competitive, and be an employer of choice for the region. More businesses should have that same goal. Here are a few action steps you should put in place:

- Institute transformational leadership techniques in your organization;

- Communicate more and provide direction;

- Manage the talent of your people;

- Identify and exterminate "organizational pathologies";

- Innovate and manage the ideas of your workforce;

- Keep your people engaged and energized; and

- Emotionally connect with your customers.

12

Leaders Energize and Engage the Workforce

We can't merely employ someone's hands and tell him to leave his heart, mind and spirit at home. Today's workers are looking for many things in an employment relationship. They want a meaningful partnership with their workplaces. Workplaces that provide meaning and purpose and are fun, engaging and energizing will enjoy greater retention, higher productivity and lower turnover.

A. W. "Bill" Dahlberg, the former CEO of the Southern Company, believes in having fun. At company gatherings, he has impersonated soul singer James Brown, dressed as General George Patton and arrived decked out as a fortune-teller, complete with crystal ball.

Employees at PeopleSoft Inc. remember the day CEO David Duffield danced the "Macarena" in front of 500 energized co-workers.

At Odetics Inc., they're still talking about the time the chief technology officer took over duty on the cafeteria cash register on St. Patrick's Day, dressed as a leprechaun!

And then there's John Briggs, a former executive at Yahoo! In early 1997, Briggs promised sales people he would have the Web directory's logo tattooed on his posterior when the company's stock passed $50 a share. To show he had kept his promise, he modeled the new tattoo in front of everyone in the company.

Finally, there's something called "Bowling with Turkeys." Hotel tradition calls for employees at the Hyatt Regency (Lexington, Ky.) to wrap a 12-pound frozen turkey with electrical tape, then roll it 50 feet down the loading dock and try to turn over as many wine bottle "bowling pins" as possible. Winners get a pumpkin pie.

After a professional lifetime identifying what it takes to transform ordinary organizations into extraordinary places to work, I know work can be awfully boring—unless someone at the top shakes everything up.

The leaders and organizations I just mentioned know it is important to engage, energize and involve people in their work. You need to lighten up and have some fun every now and then.

It isn't hard to dress up as a leprechaun, sponsor a company contest, ask people for their ideas and maybe even throw a party. And the payoff for an energized work environment is enormous.

Remember Abraham Maslow? His well-known hierarchy of needs theory states all people strive for self-actualization, which is the need for innovation and creativity. When people can reach this higher level on the job they gain greater personal fulfillment, which improves job satisfaction. Yes, you still have to pay well, but an organization can create an energized, "higher calling" environment that will foster greater productivity.

Jobs and work environments using high-involvement activities provide people with autonomy, learning opportunities, meaning, purpose and a way to grow and get ahead—not to mention a host of benefits to the company as well. High-involvement activities include, but are not limited to, the use of self-managing teams, information sharing, shared goal setting, suggestion programs, brainstorming sessions, Kaizen, Idea Campaigns and motivational meetings.

A survey conducted by Development Dimensions International (DDI), asked 232 organizations around the world, including 81 from Hong Kong, Thailand, Philippines, Singapore and Indonesia, to answer the question, "Do high-performance practices improve business performance, and which practices have the greatest impact?"

The findings from the survey showed high-performance practices indeed resulted in significant improvements in all areas. Most noteworthy were the improvements in the areas of customer service and quality of the products and services. Furthermore, I would be so bold to estimate the biggest changes were not measured directly, but more implicitly. Although the survey did not measure the improvement of attitudes, retention rates and feelings of the workforce, I'm sure they improved as well.

As Maslow indicated in his theory of motivation, the more freedom people have to use their thinking ability, the more satisfaction they receive on the job and the higher they move up the pyramid of needs. People do not respond favorably to overly restrictive work environments. High-involvement activities help people reach higher levels. These places engage and energize their workforce.

13

Driving Improvement from the Bottom Up

Businesses need to look for ways to cut costs and improve performance. Capturing ideas and suggestions from employees should be a top priority.

Getting employees involved not only yields valuable ideas and suggestions, but also engages and improves employee motivation, creating a more productive and satisfying work environment. Yet many ignore the untapped resource of their employees who know their jobs better than any so-called expert.

Marsha Myers of Lee Hecht Harrison said, "Managers usually overlook the company's most valuable asset and source of information—their employees. As the economy slows, creative organizations can find new ways to drive revenue and reduce costs by seeking employee suggestions."

Fact 1: Just 41 percent of employees think their senior management supports new ideas and new ways of doing things.

Fact 2: Only 44 percent of employees think their organization's employee suggestion program is effective.

Source: Chart Your Course International Job Satisfaction Survey

With these facts in mind, let me outline a few effective employee suggestion programs.

Study after study show most suggestion programs fail to work as intended. Many organizations still use suggestion boxes. But for many people a suggestion box is an extinct dinosaur of the past. Why?

Employees have learned most suggestions just sit in the box and go unanswered. Then there is this situation that occurred recently. A company president sent an e-mail to all his employees asking them to send him their ideas.

Employees responded and sent in dozens of ideas and suggestions. The president was impressed, but overwhelmed. Because there was no infrastructure in place to evaluate and implement the ideas, most of the suggestions withered and died along with the attitudes and trust of his employees.

During the past 30 years, I have worked with hundreds of organizations in designing employee suggestion and engagement programs. Years ago, I was responsible for creating an employee suggestion program for an organization of 72,000 people. As a board member of the Malcolm Baldrige National Quality Award, I had the opportunity to examine and evaluate how leading organizations use their Employee Suggestion Systems (ESS) to produce results. I trained managers at Yamaha and learned how they drive continuous improvement with their Kaizen process. My experiences have taught me what works and what does not. Here are a few programs to consider.

Good Idea Boards

Atlanta's Buckhead Ritz-Carlton Hotel collects ideas and suggestions by asking employees to write them on an "easy wipe" board in their respective departments. Instead of passing untested ideas up the chain of command, the employee who originates an idea has responsibility for its implementation. They follow a three-step work process: "Study it, pilot it and adopt it."

Each department has a quality coach to help individuals with their ideas and suggestions. Once an idea is piloted and found worthwhile, it is adopted. Each department forwards the best idea to the division and then on to the Quality Office for special recognition each month.

Continuous Improvement Process (CIP)

Wainwright Industries Inc. designed its suggestion program and began capturing 300 ideas a week from its workforce. In the early 1990s they implemented over 8,400 improvement ideas. The associates—not management—manage this powerful process. It works because associates at Wainwright have authority to make any improvements, without getting approval, up to $1,000 in cost. If their idea exceeds this amount, they fill out a form for approval. The names of individuals who submitted ideas are randomly drawn for a cash award each month. The company conducts quarterly drawings for a $300 gift certificate, and it comes with a catered luncheon for everyone who submitted a CIP during that quarter.

Idea Expositions

The Sony Corporation is known for its ability to create and manufacture new and innovative products. Each year they generate approximately 1,000 new products and product improvements. In order to foster the exchange of ideas within departments, Sony sponsors an annual Idea Exposition. Scientists and engineers display projects and ideas they are developing. Open only to Sony's employees, the exposition lets individuals share ideas with each other to promote cross-fertilization between departments and divisions.

Bright Ideas Campaign

The Bright Ideas Campaign is a streamlined and powerful variant to typical suggestion programs. With most suggestion box programs, results are sporadic and slow. Many good ideas get screened out, lay dormant or are overlooked and ignored by management. On the other hand, this high-intensity campaign generates hundreds of ideas in three weeks or less.

The Bright Ideas Campaign is based on a military-style operation designed to focus on specific improvement opportunities. Employees are asked to submit ideas on one or more of these areas:

1. Cost reduction

2. Continuous improvement

3. Problem identification

4. Customer retention and satisfaction

5. New product and service generation

The goal is to get one idea from each person during each week of the campaign. Supervisors cannot say "no" to any idea. Each one is evaluated and every participant receives instant recognition for the idea they submit. After the initial three-week period, employees continue to provide ideas and suggestions for continuous improvement.

WIKA, a German-owned company located in Lawrenceville, Ga., captured over 1,600 ideas from 600 employees in just three weeks. One suggestion alone was worth over $125,000 in cost savings.

14

How to Develop an Effective Incentive Program

Disney World has over 20 reward and incentive programs in place. All good businesses have at least one or two. Incentive programs serve a specific purpose. Some programs show appreciation to employees. Others are designed to improve performance and create behaviors management would like to see. No matter what type of program you have or want, designing the program is critical to its success.

Step 1: Focus on the desired behavior or the goal of the program. Begin with a clear, briefly stated objective. Identify what goal or objective needs to be accomplished, for example, improved attendance, longevity or reduced accidents. The objectives must be specific, simple and obtainable.

Step 2: Select an implementation team. Before advancing, set up a committee of employees to obtain recommendations from the people who actually will be affected by the recognition effort. It is important to bring people in from all levels of the organization. Use an outside expert if necessary to facilitate the process. Ensure the team helps to set the goals, performance factors and are in a position to report any obstacles to improvement.

Step 3: Outline a strategy. Build the foundation of the incentive program carefully. Decide on the methodology to be used. Focus on and detail who is the target audience, and anyone else who will be affected by the program. Decide if the program is going to be employee or management driven. Employee-driven programs are the best and easiest to carry out.

Step 4: Decide on the budget. Ensure there are adequate resources available before starting the program. A program involving sales personnel will be different and usually costs more money.

Step 5: Set goals. Establish quantifiable and qualitative goals that can be measured. Try to keep it as simple as possible. The more complicated, the more likely this effort will fail. The goals need to be fair and reachable for the target group.

Step 6: Pick the type of recognition or award. It is important to select the correct award. The power and influence of the award/recognition is minimized if the individual does not care about receiving it. Spend time discussing with the target group and select an award within the budget framework. You may select several types of awards or recognition and allow the winners to choose.

Step 7: Develop a communication strategy. Most programs fail due to poor communication. How will people know about the program? Decide what form or forms of media to use such as a newsletter, e-mail, a brochure or in new employee orientation materials? Decide how to remind people through the lifecycle of the program.

Step 8: Implement the program. The best programs are those the employees run themselves. On the other hand, management-directed programs usually take more energy and enthusiasm to carry out. After a couple months, time requirements are reduced. The target group will need consistent and clear communication on the results and measurement of the intended behavior and performance.

Step 9: Create a meaningful presentation strategy. This is critical to the program's overall success. The best planning can fail miserably if the presentation strategy is poorly executed. Decide on either a formal or informal presentation. Be creative and award recipients with as much fanfare as possible. Involve top executives in the presentation strategy.

Step 10: Improve and change the program. The job of the implementation team is not over until they evaluate the program. Did it achieve its objectives and goals? Were the participants motivated to change their behavior? All incentive programs have a limited lifetime. Begin planning for the next program.

15

Energize Your Employee of the Month Program

Few Employee of the Month (EOM) programs work as intended. The results fall short and, in some cases, the program does more harm than good. Why?

Fairness is the main problem. Any program that selects only one winner is bound to make others feel like losers. Another limitation is employees must be nominated for consideration. So what happens to people whose manager does not take the time to nominate anyone? What happens to people who telecommute or work outside the traditional work environment? Honoring one person also defeats the concept of teamwork. To encourage and reward teamwork, consider modifying your program.

One organization we worked with was not happy with their EOM program. Every month one person was nominated for selection. Part of the difficulty was that person had to compete against people working in eight different branch offices. A committee of eight senior managers, one from each building, selected only one winner. The winner was given a cash award.

I found several weaknesses with the program. First, the winners felt uncomfortable winning the award. They realized there were others just as deserving as they were. Second, those who were not nominated felt ignored or that they were not appreciated. Then there were others who felt the managers were playing favorites and you had to "brown nose" your boss in order to win. The program seemed to create more bad feelings than good. Something had to change.

The organization followed our recommendation to allow the employees the opportunity to redesign a better program. We convened a problem-solving team consisting of one volunteer from each branch. At the first meeting, we outlined the options the team could consider. Then we let them go to work.

An hour or two later they came up with a remake of the program. Instead of allowing the managers to decide, they implemented a peer selection process. Each branch would run a separate EOM program. Then they decided to collect money to buy a plaque for each building to display winners' names. Finally, the staff would take the winner out for breakfast each month and provide them a reserved parking space near the front door. The end result was a program allowing maximum participation and costing less to run and manage. Everyone gained from the process.

16

Why Good Companies Fail

Have you ever experienced this in your company? Company X celebrated its 20th anniversary this year. During those 20 years many things have changed. Once a shining star in their industry, now they were fading fast.

The human resources director was the first person to bring up the problem. It seemed the executives were going one way and everyone else was moving in the opposite direction. Over the past 12 months they implemented two realignments and laid off 20 percent of the workforce. Employees complained they were working the jobs of two people and cited a lack of communication and a growing frustration and distrust of management. People reported the leadership direction appeared reactionary and disjointed. The HR director tried to explain the problem to the president of the company, but it became apparent the meeting was not going anywhere.

When we entered the picture, I requested a meeting with the president. After I asked a few questions the picture became clear. He had been in his position for eight months and was brought in to turn things around. It seemed the harder he pushed, the worse things became. His frustration was palpable. His executive leadership team was not working together, and in fact, one of his executives was sabotaging the process. The combined frustration had caused him many sleepless nights, high blood pressure and was affecting his home life. If the company did not turn the corner soon they would ultimately face bankruptcy and disgrace.

Jim Collins' latest book, "How the Mighty Fall," describes the five stages of decline this company was experiencing.

Stage 1: Hubris born of success
During this stage the company begins losing sight of the values and strategies that made it successful. Its success becomes a weakness that begins to eat away at the foundation, and a feeling of entitlement permeates the organization.

Stage 2: Undisciplined pursuit of more
The organization has the feeling it can do no wrong. It behaves as if it is invincible and is blind to its incompetence. The organization expands into markets and executives make risky and undisciplined decisions to grow, purchase, expand and enter into areas about which they know little and should not be involved.

Stage 3: Denial of risk and peril
As they enter this stage, warning signs and metrics begin to mount. Teamwork, communication and morale issues begin to surface. Despite the symptoms, the organization ignores reality and continues along the path of destruction.

Stage 4: Grasping for salvation
At this stage, it is struggling and looking for a silver bullet solution to save them. Typical reactions can include bringing in

a new charismatic CEO, implementing bold and daring new strategies and making new acquisitions and radical transformations. The clock is ticking and unless it gets the right help at this stage, it has little chance of recovering.

Stage 5: Capitulation to irrelevance and death

So what do you do if you find yourself in this predicament? The good news is if you catch the decline in the early stages, then most companies can remedy the problem themselves. But when the problem has gone on for a lengthy amount of time, when the Band-Aids, silver bullet programs and flavor du jour have failed to work, then you may need outside assistance. The longer you wait, the more difficult the cure. It is similar to a patient who keeps experiencing a pain that never goes away. When he finally goes to the doctor, the treatment ends up costing a lot more money in lost opportunities, time and inconvenience.

I have learned an "outsider" has a special ability to address and talk openly about business matters that an "insider" cannot. The old proverb, "It is lonely at the top," is true. Executives can share things with me they will never share with others in the company. This position of trust is sacred and the objective and honest feedback is critical.

A couple of weeks after my first meeting with the new president of Company X, the executive team met off site for a daylong meeting. The executive team was comprised of intelligent, dedicated and motivated individuals. However, each one had a completely different personality, values and opinions about how to lead their company out of the mess. They were able to lay everything on the table—no holds barred.

At the end of this meeting, they had outlined a unified strategy, with goals and action steps to move forward. Now after several months, the company has turned the corner and mostly everyone is pleased with the direction they are going.

III

Creating a Great Place to Work

17
People First, Employees Second

Lou Kaucic recently retired as the executive vice president and chief people officer at Applebee's International. Kaucic began developing retention programs using a comprehensive human resource system called "People Metrics," an initiative that has helped to lower employee turnover dramatically. As a result he was named to Human Resource Executive Magazine's Human Resources Honor Roll.

Because of these programs, the turnover rate among store managers had fallen to eight percent. Kaucic discovered it costs $10,000 to replace and train restaurant managers. Turnover for all unit-level managers is around 14 percent annually, an astonishingly low figure in an industry where a 50-percent turnover rate remains the norm for management positions.

Employee retention begins by hiring the right people. Studies show restaurants with the lowest turnover rates have the strongest managers. As part of the hiring process, management candidates have four or five job interviews. They only get the job if their skills match established competencies, which include decision-making, integrity, employee retention and managing relationships.

No one wants to work for a bad boss. So they put in place a thorough annual review process to identify both low- and high-performing managers. Applebee's has over 2,000 managers in more than 400 restaurants. The process is called "Mix Management" and it assesses managers based on nine competencies. Once in place, the system gave Kaucic a way to organize managers into three groups: the top 20 percent, the middle 60 percent and the bottom 20 percent. Once supervisors saw the breakdown and identified top- and mid-range performers, they went to work retaining them. The top 20 percent were identified as future leaders within the company. The bottom 20 percent consists of new managers and those who may be in the wrong job. Those individuals are given the choice to improve or leave.

Turnover Alert Form

Applebee's provides a generous bonus program and a benefit package that treats managers as "people first, employees second," as Kaucic says. During their quarterly People Metrics meetings, managers share ideas and best practices for employee retention.

One practice they put in place is something called a Turnover Alert Form. The process identifies and attempts to prevent discontented managers from quitting. In several situations, Applebee's has flown the managers to meet with the CEO and possibly other executives. They want to identify and repair anything that might be causing job dissatisfaction.

Like the managers, hourly workers participate in a similar evaluation process. Applebee's created assessment tools focused on helping managers evaluate hourly employees based on another set of nine core competencies such as punctuality, stamina, teamwork and appearance. This is a two-part rating process. Associates grade themselves every six months and their restaurant manager also scores them. As a result, the evaluation process breaks their workforce into the top 80 percent and the bottom 20 percent. The manager then decides either to keep those employees in the bottom group or let them go.

18

Managing Talent and Driving High Performance

Can you imagine a professional football coach hiring just anyone as quarterback? How many games would the team lose before the coach is fired? The truth is many businesses do just that. They hire the first person who walks through the door and then wonder why performance drops and good employees quit.

Talent management is the process that finds the best talent affordable. It allows good employees to stay as long as possible, and encourages mismatched employees to leave sooner or to find more compatible jobs elsewhere.

Who is the top talent in your organization? Is it the person who is the one paid the highest or the least? Is the server more important to the success of the restaurant or is it the CEO? So, while you might want to invest more dollars for high-priced, high-profile, hard-to-replace executives, it is important to spend time, effort and money on everyone.

I have identified eight basic elements essential to creating a talent management organization. While each one, like the sails of a ship, can harness the power of the wind, all eight are needed for proper navigation. A sail not properly set hinders the progress of the ship and causes frustration among the crew members.

1. Clear sense of direction and purpose

Everyone wants to be paid for what he does, but good employees also want to be part of an organization that stands for something and gives them personal fulfillment and meaning. When an organization means something, people are willing to give more. That is why they work for nonprofit organizations or spend their off-work hours leading Scout troops and building houses for Habitat for Humanity.

2. Caring management

Interpersonal skills are an essential element of the high-retention culture. People want to feel management cares and is concerned for them as individuals. Yet poor "soft skills" are one of the biggest factors that drive people away.

3. Flexible benefits and schedules adapted to the needs of the individual

Flexibility rules in today's workplace. The one-size-fits-all approach to benefits has long since lost its effectiveness. Workers will migrate to a company whose benefit packages and schedules help them meet the demands of their lives, whether they are single parents, adults who care for aging parents, older workers, younger workers, part-time workers or telecommuters.

4. Open communication

People have a large appetite for information, and they want it instantly. High-retention workplaces put high priority on delivering the right information to the right people at the right time using the right methodology. Companies who leave employees in the dark risk damaging morale and motivation—not to mention compromising their ability to make a quick course change in the marketplace.

5. Charged work environment

People want to enjoy their work. They shun boring, bureaucratic, lifeless work environments. That is why high-performance workplaces do not bother with the traditional ways of doing things. They find new ways to make work mentally engaging and physically energizing. They also ask for, listen to and implement the ideas and suggestions of those who work for them.

6. Performance management

It is a challenge to find competent, motivated workers who have good attitudes and work ethics. Because of this, knowing how to manage performance is important. Performance management includes a new set of skills, tools, techniques and processes to align an individual and his behavior with the goals of the business enterprise.

7. Reward and recognition

All humans need to feel appreciated. Reward and recognition programs help meet that need. A workplace that rewards and recognizes people builds higher productivity and loyalty, and can create consequences for desired behavior that leads to organizational success.

8. Training and development

Many workers just want a paycheck, but the best workers want opportunity. They want to develop their skills and potential and to enhance their ability to contribute and succeed. Training and development give people greater control and ownership over their jobs, making them capable of taking care of customers and creating better management-employee relationships.

19

Flexible Work Arrangements Help Retain Good People

Balancing work and family has received a lot of attention over the years for several reasons. First, today's workforce is increasingly diverse and demanding. Second, the workforce is shrinking. There are not enough skilled workers to fill all the jobs.

In this country skilled workers have options. It is important not to force workers to choose between work and family. Each year thousands of good people leave good jobs to take other positions that are more family-friendly. This situation has fueled the dramatic rise of home-based and female-owned businesses.

A one-size-fits-all approach no longer works. Employers must either accommodate the needs of their people or be faced with constant turnover and unhappy employees.

The cost of turnover is much more expensive than people realize. In the U.S. it costs between $7,000 and $17,000 to replace an hourly employee, upwards to $40,000 to replace a manager, and even more to replace a senior level executive.

In spite of the staggering cost, the majority of businesses do not have a formal retention program.

What makes one person happy can be the very thing that displeases another. That is why organizations must pay specific attention to the various needs and expectations each person may have.

By creating a Flexible Work Arrangement (FWA), companies can keep good employees and not force them to sacrifice the diverse needs of their family life. An FWA will help them benefit personally and professionally, and the result will be people who are more loyal, committed and productive.

FWAs offer options to employees who do not want or need a standard work schedule. A properly prepared FWA allows greater flexibility in balancing roles of work and home. It also can help prevent valuable employees from quitting and taking a less suitable position elsewhere. Most of the time, FWAs involve fewer work hours and possibly a proportional reduction of pay and benefits.

A survey by Flexible Resources Inc. of more than 500 women seeking flexible work arrangements found that 64 percent of them had either quit or were planning to quit due to the lack of work hour flexibility. What was alarming was that 59 percent of these women never asked their employers to modify their work schedules because they assumed they would be denied or lose stature. Younger women are more assertive in seeking flexible work arrangements; 72 percent of women between the ages of 25 and 35 were willing to request an FWA compared to only 30 percent of the women ages 36 to 45.

Among those who requested a Flexible Work Arrangement and were told "no," reasons for the refusal ran the gamut in the following priority:

- We can't give it to you and not the others (52 percent)
- You will not be available to others (48 percent)
- We have never done it before (24 percent)
- You won't be as productive as when you work full time (8 percent)
- Your job is not conducive to flexible hours (5 percent)
- There is too much work to do (5 percent)
- It wouldn't fit into a team atmosphere (5 percent)

But FWAs do have drawbacks. People feel physical presence equals more opportunity for promotions and advancement. Men are particularly vulnerable to the stigma, "if you are not at work full time, you are not competitive."

Several years ago Working Mother magazine recognized the innovative work/life programs provided by the Bank of America. Its "Child Care Plus" program pays eligible workers an additional amount of money each week per child for employees earning less than $30,000 a year. BOA learned that turnover for participants was about half that of the peer group not participating. So they expanded the program to include workers with family incomes of $60,000 and also began to allow workers two paid hours a week to work in their children's schools. Finally, they added money for college. Bank of America gives $2,000 a year for employees enrolled in undergraduate classes and $4,000 for graduate study. As a result, they were able to reduce turnover by 50 percent.

20

Motivating and Retaining the Younger Workforce

The younger generation brings major new challenges to the labor market. They want and demand benefits such as stock option plans, health care insurance, and time off (paid vacation, sick days and personal leave days). They tend to be less motivated by promises of overtime pay and more motivated by personal satisfaction with their jobs. The No. 1 benefit for younger employees is development and training. They want to grow in their jobs, learn new skills and reach a higher level of potential.

Unlike their parents and grandparents, younger employees do not anticipate staying with one job or company throughout their entire career. They have seen their parents laid off. Many of them have grown up in divorced family situations. They expect to change jobs as they seek employment that offers them both better benefits and more opportunity for professional growth as well as personal fulfillment.

They want, and expect, their employers to hear what they have to say. They have an interest in understanding the "big picture" for the company and how this influences their employment and growth. They are less likely to accept a "be-cause-I-said-so" attitude from a supervisor.

What can you do to motivate these employees for maximum productivity? Five general areas come to mind.

1. Take time to be personal.
Thank an employee for doing a good job (in person, in writing, or both). Listen to what employees have to say, both in a one-on-one situation and in group meetings.

2. Encourage employee growth.
Provide feedback on the employee's performance. Be specific, mentioning a particular situation or activity. Make sure the employee understands company expectations. Involve them in the decision-making process whenever possible. Let them know what happened to the idea or suggestion they submitted. Give an employee room to do the job without unnecessary restrictions. Pay for employees to attend workshops and seminars; offer on-site classes where employees can learn new skills or improve upon old ones. Most jobs contain a certain amount of routine and day-to-day work, so offer employees a chance to work on something in which they have a special interest, something that will challenge them.

3. Reward and recognize superior performance.
Recognize an employee who has done an outstanding job by giving an unexpected reward, such as a day off or a free dinner for the employee and his family at a nice restaurant. Do not penalize an employee who is doing such a great job in their present situation that you do not want him or her to move to a new position. The employee who deserves the

promotion and does not get it will likely look elsewhere for a better opportunity outside the organization.

4. Help employees understand how the business operates.

Employees need to experience a sense of ownership. Encourage this by providing them with information about new products, advertising campaigns or strategies for competing. Let each employee see how he fits into the plan. Help them see how meeting their goals contribute to meeting the organization's goals.

5. Build morale.

Have an open work environment; encourage initiative and welcome new ideas. Don't be afraid to spend a few dollars for such things as free coffee for employees, M&Ms or ordering a meal for employees who have to work overtime. Take time to speak with an employee's spouse or family when you meet them and let them know you appreciate the employee.

Remember, they look for more than just fair pay: they need and want personal acknowledgment and job satisfaction.

21

Does The "Deli Lama" Work Here?

The right job titles provide status and self-esteem and can help you reduce turnover and improve pride.

People care about their job titles. Sometimes they will even choose the better title over more pay. A recent graduate with a desire to move up in a chosen career field may feel acquiring a title that will look good on their resume is worth accepting a little less money. Recruiters have discovered they receive a better response with well-chosen job titles. Administrative assistant or sales associate are boring, bureaucratic and easy to skip over in the classifieds. "Chief of client relations" will attract much more attention.

The president of a computer service company once tried an experiment: He offered new hires at a remote location a choice between the title of sales manager or salesperson. Although the salesperson position paid $2,000 a year more, most people took the manager title.

A bicycle storeowner asked me what he could do to keep his best employee from quitting. He could not afford to give him a big raise. I said, "Give him a small raise and then ask him what job title he would like." It turned out the title the employee wanted was "director of bike operations" (DBO). Problem solved. The job title changed his attitude about his job and sounded impressive to his friends too.

Director of bike operations has terrific ego appeal. People want to be proud of their job titles. A grocery store chain allowed the delicatessen manager to choose his title and he is now called the "Deli Lama." We have to get over the bureaucratic concept that only certain people get certain job titles and business cards. Allow a little freedom of choice and you will reap plenty in loyalty.

The ultimate goal is to energize people and make them feel good about their jobs. If it is a choice between losing a good employee and a job title, I would go with the job title every time, especially because giving an employee a prestigious title is one way to recognize and reward him when a raise is not affordable. Here are a few job title examples we have seen:

- Senior Vice President of Great People
- Chief Talent Scout
- Director of Fun
- Director of Consumer Delight
- Top Dog
- Person in Charge
- Top Employee No. 1

Here are a few other ideas to consider:

Invent a new job.

A 12-year veteran at Charles Schwab was considering leaving the company until his boss allowed him to invent a new job as organizational troubleshooter that drew on his technical and business skills. Now a vice president in Schwab's Electronic Brokerage group, he acknowledges that creating his own job let him "change things and get charged up about work again," and calls it "the key to my staying."

Encourage hallway training.

A study to see how much information co-workers shared informally demonstrated that during a typical week at one company, over 70 percent of the 1,000 workers in the study shared information with fellow employees. Fifty-five percent asked co-workers for advice. This spontaneous exchange took place during meetings; exchanges with customers, supervisors, and mentors; on-the-job training; site visits; cross-training; shift changes; same-level employee communication; and simply doing one's job. The next time you see employees talking during shift changes, in the halls or at coffee breaks, remember you may be witnessing learning in progress.

Use "stand-ups" to reinforce company culture.

The Ritz-Carlton Hotels have always made training and development a top priority. Today, Ritz-Carlton practices something called "stand-ups" before each shift. All employees across the globe receive a 10- to 15-minute class on the same topic. The shift leader inspects each employee for proper uniform, nametag and appearance. The stand-up will include a review of one of the Ritz-Carlton's 20 customer service basics. The stand-up concludes with announcements and a discussion of guest preferences, and then everyone is ready to begin their shift.

Chick-fil-A University

Chick-fil-A is a popular restaurant chain. Its turnover rates are one of the lowest in the fast food restaurant industry as the result of its commitment to training. Through its Chick-Fil-A University, new store owners, called operators, benefit from a comprehensive seven-week training program. Store managers attend classes for three weeks in Atlanta and then two weeks of training take place in the field. After a one-week reinforcement phase, operators spend five days at their restaurant working with a coach from corporate headquarters who helps them solve problems and review everything they learned during the seven-week process.

22

Case Study – Seton Health – A Great Place to Work

Kathleen Occhiogrosso is Vice President of Human Resources at Seton Health located in Troy, New York. As part of their ongoing management strategy, they focus on enhanced communication, professional growth and development and having fun in their workplace. It's a cumulative combination of these initiatives that make Seton Health a good place to work.

Seton Health's 2008 Engagement Survey ranked them among the top five facilities within their national healthcare system. The local Capital District Business Review also designated them as one the "Best Places to Work."

Communication

They conduct leadership rounds on all units and departments in the organization. Senior leaders pair up and visit departments on a rotating basis and ask questions such as:

- What is working well?
- What is not working?
- What are your daily frustrations?

■ Who or what other department would you like to recognize that has been especially helpful to you?

■ Are there any safety issues we should know about?

During the rounds, they take notes and their senior leaders ensure all issues get logged and are followed up. They also encourage and respond to all employee suggestions received through their suggestion program. Suggestions and responses are placed on their internal e-mail system and in the company employee newsletter so all employees know their voice is heard.

Seton Health created an "Operations Council," which is a select group of directors and managers who meet every other month to assist senior leaders with workplace issues. They hold manager group meetings on the opposite month so all managers stay informed and have a formal communication venue.

They hold quarterly employee roundtable discussions. About 10 to 15 employees from a cross-section of departments are invited on a rotating basis to an intimate meeting with the COO and the VP of Human Resources to discuss anything on their minds.

Senior leadership meets with newly hired employees at six months of employment to just check in with them and to make sure things are going well. This is important to ensure any problems are addressed early on in their employment. Their own managers, though in contact on a daily basis, formally meet with them at 30 and 90 days from their start date.

Professional growth and development

They provide generous tuition reimbursement for all job-related degrees. They cover expenses for job-related certifications and provide a generous student loan forgiveness program for hard-to-fill positions such as nursing, medical imaging and physical therapy.

Seton Health's School-At-Work Program allows their entry-level associates to train and build a career path in health care. They are given paid time off from their regular job to get on-site training and education in medical terminology, math and working with computers. They have had two groups of six students go through the program. All have graduated and some have already been placed in higher level positions within their system.

They have enrolled managers in local leadership development programs offered in the community. Additionally, they provide growth opportunities within their system for managers to gain new skills in areas outside their normal responsibilities.

Fun in the workplace

They try to have fun in the workplace. Each year they have a theme party. In 2009, in lieu of holding a more expensive annual theme party, they held a "Sock Hop Day," which included a 1950's-era costume contest. As part of the event they held a hula-hoop contest during the lunch period and created a special menu including sliders, fries and milkshakes with 1950's music playing in the background. Members of senior management handed out free milkshakes to employees and visitors. It was a low-cost way to thank employees and show they are committed to having fun in the workplace. Despite having to make the cutbacks, the employees understood the reasons and supported the decision.

The above strategies are just a few examples of what they do on a regular basis to retain their employees and ensure they have a voice. As a result, their employee turnover continues to decrease and they have an 18 percent re-hire rate, meaning that 18 percent of their new hires are employees who left and decided to come back. Their engagement survey scores continue to increase year-after-year. They focus on retention at all times, both in periods of financial downturn as well as during more favorable financial times.

23

Tips to Get People Fired Up

Terry Deal, business professor at Vanderbilt University in Nashville, Tenn., noted companies which allow some play in the workplace realize higher profits.

Here are a few new tips you can adapt to help you create a more productive and motivated work environment.

Gold stars and frogs
Each Monday morning, Wachovia Bank sets milestones for the week with input from staff members. On Fridays, employees receive a gold star and $2 (funny money) for each milestone met. Employees can also recognize their peers with a sticker of a frog, which is worth $1. Staff members display the gold stars and frogs on a white cardboard poster. At the end of each month, they hold a random drawing for a dinner ($50.00) and movies ($25.00).

Generate competition
Here is a tip from the U.S. Air Force: Once each quarter the wing commander recognizes the airman, NCO (non-commissioned officer) and Senior NCO of the quarter at a Commander's Call. Nominations come from within each

unit, which then works to support their nominee, thereby generating competition between units.

Birthday Club

Energize your employees with fun! Once a month hold a Birthday Club celebration. At break time, have special goodies and recognize employees who have a birthday that month with a card.

Reward good health

At Cornell University, an Excellent Attendance Program rewards employees who do not use a sick day during a six-month period with a day off, plus a certificate of recognition given at a special luncheon.

Improve quality, cost and performance

Employees at Melrose Company who submit ideas to improve quality, cost and performance are eligible for a $90 gift certificate to Wal-Mart. During a yearly banquet for all contributors, the company also gives larger cash awards and items such as televisions.

Work to earn time off

Employees at Grayson College Golf Course who did not miss a day of work for three weeks received a day off, which they could use on days when bad weather meant the course was not busy.

Butts for Balls

At Pine Oaks Golf Course, employees receive one bag of range balls for picking up one cup of cigarette butts.

A work of art at NASA

A graphics artist makes caricatures of individuals and groups of people and uses the artwork as awards. Team members proudly display them on their desks. Eventually, everyone on the team gets a picture.

Create an Employee Activity Fund

Here's a tip from the U.S. Navy: Use an annual "auction" to raise employee activity funds. They auction off various items such as a round of golf. They funds raised from the auction are used for office functions and activities.

24

LaRosa's Puts People First

The service and food industry experiences some of the highest employee turnover rates of all industries in the United States. The reasons for this are varied, but can be attributed to low pay, long hours and weekends.

However, one company clearly stands out above the rest. LaRosa's is a national chain of over 50 outlets consisting of 3,000 employees with over $100 million in sales each year.

LaRosa's practices the art of leadership and takes the science of quality management to its highest form. The first major difference between this company and other food businesses is they consider their employees their internal customers. They spend as much time and energy focusing on their internal customers as their external customers. Putting their people first is like the law of physics: for every action there is an equal and opposite reaction. In this case, the reaction is a higher level of customer service provided to their external customers, which in turn generates higher profits.

In most businesses the human resources department is responsible for people issues. The problem experienced in most American companies is the HR manager is only holding a staff position. Unfortunately, in some cases, most HR departments do not have the power or respect to make change. The power to make change rests with the people who have the authority.

The philosophy is different at LaRosa's. Their Chairman of the Board Tillman Hughes says, "The soft stuff needs to become the 'hard stuff.'"

Most businesses pay only lip service when it comes to taking care of their employees. However, it goes from lip service to reality when you actually measure it. This puts a company in a powerful position to make improvements and hold people accountable. At LaRosa's they use several different measurement methods.

Managers meet with new hired workers for the first four weeks and conduct a new hire survey approximately 30 days after they have been on board. Then they ask questions such as, "How do you feel about working here?" and "How is training going?"

Managers conduct a cultural audit once a year. The audit measures the feelings employees' have about pay and benefits, reward and recognition and how they feel about the company. This gives management a quick pulse on how employees feel about how they are being treated.

Employees also evaluate their bosses. They conduct a bottom-up Internal Customer Satisfaction Index (ICSI) twice a year with all employees. The ICSI has only four questions and asks the employee to give their manager a letter grade from A to D in four categories:

Communication: Use of basic principles, effective method used/established for verbal and written messages or instructions, feedback provided or allowed, Code of Conduct honored.

Accountability: Timeliness, maintains schedules, facilitates the workflow, responsiveness.

Quality: Provides quality work and/or service (i.e.: accurate information, support documentation, quality products etc.).

Professionalism: Exhibits courtesy and professionalism. The individual handles situations in a responsible and mature manner. Effectively communicates and delivers quality products/service resulting in total Team Member Satisfaction.

After the ICSI is completed and the comments have been tabulated, the CEO has the managers come in and talk about the results. They address specific behaviors and come up with action plans for improvement that can be tracked daily. The meetings are held in an open and trusting environment so not to cause any fear of retaliation.

LaRosa's also discovered leadership training is a key to their success. At one time, the company sent managers to those public, one-day leadership courses downtown. Executives found it was hard to reach critical mass because everyone came back with different ideas, a different philosophy and a different language of what leadership meant. LaRosa's now sends all its managers to the same six-week training program.

25

The Friendly Factor
Gets People Engaged

It should go without saying if you cannot attract and keep your workforce, then you must change what you are doing or face the consequences.

Which type of place would you want to work: One that is cold and gives you a sense that no one cares, or one that makes you feel good and appreciated? Money and benefits are important, but studies show in the long run the work environment— the feeling they get when they come to work— is more important to retaining and motivating people.

People like a friendly place to work. The friendly-factor does not require a large investment and expense, but it does require time and thoughtful consideration. Take for example a construction equipment dealership in Louisville, Ky.

The employees and service technicians participate in a profit-sharing plan that could possibly mean $700,000 upon retirement. They are eligible to participate after one year and become fully vested after six years. No one has quit after becoming vested in this company. To further help his employees, the owner brings in a financial advisor to help them select stocks, plan for retirement or to provide advice on buying a house or saving for a child's college education.

Employees celebrate their work anniversary with a cake. They also receive specific amount of money for each year employed, made out in a check so they can buy work tools for the shop.

Twice a year the employees children receive a $50 savings bond when the child brings in their "all A's" report card.

This company rewards employees' safety records with what they call a Safety Bonus Program. They screen each employee's driving record twice a year. Anyone who has a citation during the year is removed from the program. At the end of the year, the ones who remain get to split $2,000.

To minimize the "we/they" syndrome, the employees rotate jobs every Friday. The person in the Parts Department gets to be a service technician and vice versa. This builds a stronger team and improves communication within the company.

Here are a few other friendly-factor ideas to consider:

■ During your new employee orientation, make sure you send a welcome gift or letter to the family of the new employee welcoming them to the company. Assign the new employee a mentor to help them adjust to the new environment and make them feel part of the team. After their first 30 days on the job, have a new employee celebration and invite their family members to attend.

- Be involved in the important aspects of your employees' lives. You should respond when there is a birth, illness, death, graduation or wedding. These are the important events where you have a golden opportunity to build a bond between the individual and the company.

- One company photographed each employee who had worked at the company over five years. Then they put the photos on a wall for all to see. This small act built a bond and showed the employees the pride their employer had in them.

- Have a "Bring children to work day." Perhaps twice a year allow your employees to bring their kids and show them what they do.

Creating a friendly-factor work environment takes time, and it takes managers who truly care about individuals.

26

People Need To Feel Appreciated

Susan had worked in the Quality Assurance department for months. In addition to doing her job well, she voluntarily came in early each day and had coffee ready for the rest of the team. Making coffee wasn't in her job description, but it was something she wanted to do and it made her feel good to help others. She enjoyed her job and planned to stay as long as possible.

Her supervisor, Lori, was the type of person who noticed things and always had a positive word to say. Lori even would brag about her employees in front of her district manager, Mr. Cramer.

At dinner, Susan would tell her family Lori was the reason she liked working there. Lori made her feel appreciated. Lori noticed and recognized the little things people did and always had something nice to say to them. Susan knew she could find a better paying job closer to her home, but she planned to stay as long as Lori was her boss.

Money may attract people to the front door, but something else keeps them from going out the back. Although many people claim they are quitting for a better paying job elsewhere, survey after survey shows a lack of appreciation and recognition is a primary reason why people quit their jobs.

Setting up a program to make people feel appreciated is not difficult. A well-administered program builds camaraderie and values, and makes people feel good about themselves and their jobs. But the biggest reason for the success of these programs is simple: they allow people to celebrate success and feel good about who they are and for whom they work.

27

Peer Recognition:
Employees Reward Each Other

One of the easiest and most effective programs to initiate, peer recognition gives employees the power to reward each other for doing a good job. It works because employees themselves know who works hard and deserves recognition. After all, managers can't be everywhere all the time and employees are in the best position to catch people doing the right things.

We have helped many organizations establish a peer-recognition program called "Shining Stars."

Workers have access to an unlimited supply of Shining Stars forms to hand-write a little note about the good job their co-workers are doing. On the back of the form is a list of positive behaviors such as:

- Demonstrates friendly, caring service
- Shows flexibility
- Demonstrates teamwork
- Helps save money

They complete the forms and either hand them directly to their co-worker or send them through interoffice mail. At the end of the month the organization holds a recognition ceremony for everyone recognized. The employee who received the highest number of forms gets special recognition by the team and the manager.

Then all the forms for the month are put into a basket and names are randomly drawn for additional prizes. The forms are read aloud and recognition given to both the winner as well as the person who submitted the form. The winners then randomly draw their prizes out of another basket.

These informal peer recognition programs offer several advantages over other formal recognition programs. They work best when the FAST-FUN formula is followed:

Focus on the behavior you want to reward. A peer recognition program must target specific behaviors that are important to the organization. Whether it is teamwork or customer service, define ahead of time the behavior you are looking for.

Avoid bureaucratic judging and committees. When committees and boards make decisions someone feels cheated. Charges of unfairness will surface. In the Shining Stars program and other peer recognition programs, the random drawing is a key element. Except for the person who gets the highest quantity of forms, every other "winner" is by the luck of the draw.

Simplicity. With peer recognition, the more simple the program the better. The easier the program is to run, the more likely it will work. After about six months, you may want to consider changing the program in order to maintain interest and enthusiasm.

Team ownership. Peer recognition works best when employees run and own the program. Team ownership takes the onus off the supervisor and allows the team to manage it.

FUN. Make the peer recognition program as fun, interesting and spontaneous as possible.

28

God, Car Batteries and Concern for the Family: Interstate Batteries

In my mind, a good boss is someone who acknowledges important life-changing events such as a death in the family, the birth of a child or an illness. In one of my scrapbooks is a note from my father's boss congratulating him on my birth. Today some might call this intrusive or outside the bounds of normal business, but it meant a lot to my family. And I know that similar gestures I've made for people who worked for me made a lasting impression that no bonus check could ever buy.

The modern workforce is a stressful place. What has traditionally been considered "work" and what is considered "living" are becoming blurred. Lack of job security, fractured marriages, fear, anxiety, office violence, non-stop change—all these issues are making people realize life is more than just making money. People need an anchor in their life they may have never needed before. A good boss alone may not be enough.

At the Interstate Battery System of America Inc. (IBSA), employees can turn to their employer for help in their quest for meaning. Founded in 1952 on three traditional values—offer the best-quality product, provide impeccable service and treat the customer with respect—Interstate Batteries is a $500 million, privately held corporation with more than 5,000 products. Its home office in Dallas, Texas, works with more than 300 wholesale distribution centers that service 200,000 dealers in the U.S., Canada and around the world.

Interstate takes a unique role and responsibility for its employees and family members. Management tries to make a substantial difference in people's lives beyond merely providing a place to work and a paycheck at the end of the month. Many organizations talk about caring for their employees, but Interstate demonstrates it in a number of ways.

The most notable example is its chaplain's department. Its staff of five provides and coordinates opportunities for employees to participate in pizza luncheons, men's and women's luncheons, banquets, golf tournaments, conferences and summer camps. Employees can borrow books and videos from its library, attend Bible studies, listen to guest speakers and turn to the department for personal help.

A full-time chaplain has been on Interstate's staff for the past nine years. A former Army chaplain who left the service to work at Interstate, he has helped establish many of Interstate's employee programs. The chaplain will visit family members in the hospital, attend weddings and respond to births and deaths. His office will send newly married employees to FamilyLife conferences and pick up half the tab. Employees who participate in these programs view it as a valuable aspect of working at Interstate.

Faith plays a key role at Interstate, whose mission statement calls on the company to "glorify God as we supply our customers worldwide with top quality, value-priced batteries, related electrical power-source products and distribution services." Norm Miller and other top executives hold regular prayer meetings as part of their management responsibilities and look to God for guidance in day-to-day business decisions.

Employees participate in a variety of volunteer ministries. Every quarter, about 10 spend a weekend in Bill Glass Prison Ministries' "Weekend of Champions." Interstate pays for participants' transportation, food and lodging. Twice a year, employees donate boxes of food and bags of clothing to the needy at the Union Gospel Mission. At Christmas and Easter, about 17 people participate in a prison fellowship and spend time visiting with inmates in a nearby jail.

Once a year, 100 employees participate in the Angel Tree project, which provides clothing and Christmas presents to children of prisoners. An annual mission trip to Mexico draws about 20 employees. Chairman Miller pays for the trip out of his own pocket.

Interstate recognizes employees who participate in ministry events with a Matthew 25 certificate, based on the Bible verse that says "For I was hungry and you gave Me something to eat; I was thirsty and you gave Me drink; I was a stranger and you invited Me in; I was naked and you clothed Me; I was sick and you visited Me; I was in prison and you came to Me."

It's hard to objectively measure how these programs and services impact retention and productivity. But evidence indicates employees feel Interstate truly stands for something and cares for them. This work environment is not for everyone, but for the 350 home office employees, it's ideal. As one new employee said, "I can't get over it; I feel I am a part of a family."

29

Transform Your Organization from High Turnover to High Retention

Each year U.S. businesses spend billions of dollars recruiting and replacing their employees. Individually, it costs between $7,000 and $17,000 to replace an hourly employee.

It is getting difficult to attract and keep skilled employees. Many businesses and industries are desperate for help and can't find good people with the right skills and attitudes.

While many leading companies place more effort in employee retention, many more are clueless. They accept employee turnover as a normal part of doing business. High-turnover organizations spend disproportionate amounts of resources on recruiting and replacing their workforce, while smart organizations invest in employee retention. Yes, there is going to be turnover no matter what you do, but blindly ignoring the reasons for turnover is foolish and expensive.

Just consider the turnover replacement costs by industry.

Construction	$14,500 (per employee)
Manufacturing	$14,500
Trade and Transportation	$12,500
Information	$19,500
Financial Activities	$18,000
Professional and Business	$15,500
Education and Health	$14,000
Leisure and Hospitality	$ 7,000
Other Services	$12,750
All Private	$14,000

Source: Employment Policy Foundation tabulation and analysis of Bureau of Labor Statistics, Employer Cost of Employee Compensation data.

Employees quit for many reasons but, in general, there are five important areas that motivate people to leave their jobs:

■ Poor match between the person and the job;

■ Poor fit with the organizational climate and culture;

■ Poor alignment between pay and performance;

■ Poor connections between the individual, their co-workers and the supervisor; and

■ Poor opportunities for growth and advancement.

These five P's can be addressed successfully. Employee retention begins by paying attention to what causes low job satisfaction as well as what attracts, retains and motivates your workforce.

When do you focus on employee retention?
Most businesses only focus on employee retention when turnover increases. Successful organizations make employee

retention a major part of their organizational strategy. It is something that is looked at continuously.

Here are a few items to consider:

Identify and weed out poor managers.

The relationship with the employee's front-line manager is the most common reason people leave. LaRosa's is a large restaurant business with over 3,000 employees. As part of its employee retention strategy, all employees evaluate their bosses twice a year using a special report card. It asks the employees to give their managers a letter grade from A to D in four categories. Any score less than a "B" requires a specific comment from the employee. After it's completed, they tabulate the comments and design action plans for improvement.

Hold managers accountable for turnover.

Set specific responsibilities for human resources, supervisors and executives about their specific role in employee retention. Train managers so they understand what leads to higher retention and greater job satisfaction. Hold managers responsible for retention in their departments, set turnover goals for each manager and track accordingly. Promote managers whose behavior is consistent with the organization's values and philosophies.

Create a positive work environment.

Money and benefits may bring employees through the front door, but poor work conditions drive them out the back. In its National Study of the Changing Workforce, the Families and Work Institute showed earnings and benefits have only a 3 percent impact on job satisfaction. "Job quality" and "workplace support" have a combined 70 percent on job satisfaction.

Develop an 'Onboarding' program for the first 90 days on the job.

Don't hire and abandon your new employees. Ensure they get the support, training and assistance they need. Quint Studer, CEO of the Studer Group, a consulting firm in Gulf Breeze, Fla., finds companies that take steps to "re-recruit" employees can improve performance and reduce turnover in their first three months by as much as 66 percent.

Enhance connections between co-workers, managers and the organization.

To build stronger bonds between the top management and employees, one corporate office practices something called an Employee Scavenger Hunt. Once or twice a year, they give every executive or manager five names of employees. They find each person, meet them and learn about them as individuals. The process builds a better bond, improves communication and builds trust within the organization.

Hire the best and avoid the rest.

Research shows those organizations that spend more time recruiting high-caliber people earn a 22 percent higher return to shareholders than their industry peers. Cisco CEO John Chambers said, "... a world-class engineer with five peers can out-produce 200 regular engineers." Instead of waiting for people to apply for jobs, good organizations are always on the lookout for high-caliber people.

Provide learning opportunities.

For many people, learning new skills is as important as the money they make. Identify career paths and provide developmental opportunities for employees early in their jobs with the organization. Promote ongoing, two-way communication between employees and their immediate managers regarding career progress.

TD Industries in Dallas, Texas, helps its employees feel valued by using one wall within the company to place photographs of employees who have been employed with them more than five years. They also try to make everyone feel equal and have no reserved parking spaces for executives. That is one reason why TD Industries was listed by Fortune Magazine as one of the Top 100 Best Places to Work.

Measure the attitudes of your workforce.

Fired up workplaces use employee climate assessments to measure the attitudes and feelings of their workforce. Every organization should conduct some form of climate assessment each year.

Focus on individuals.

You must manage retention one employee at a time. Focus on the key jobs that have the most impact on profitability and productivity. Everyone has a different set of needs and expectations about their jobs. By conducting an individual retention profile, managers can quickly identify the employee's unique motivations, goals, level of job satisfaction, as well as other expectations.

30

Reduce Employee Turnover of Entry Level Workers

Attracting, motivating and retaining entry-level workers can present a challenge to businesses of all sizes. The wide age range of such workers, which may include inexperienced beginners in their late teens to older workers with extensive job experience, complicates the matter. What motivates people varies according to their different needs and perceptions. Youthful workers, for example, may view the job as only a first step in their work life. Benefits, such as insurance, may not seem as important to them as to the older worker with a family.

While there may not be a magic formula for attracting and keeping entry-level workers, here are some tips to consider:

- Avoid the mindset that "it's only an entry-level job" when advertising and hiring. If you present the job as a "nothing" job, applicants will view it the same way. It may be entry-level, but it is still important to hire the best person you can find for the job.

- Pay the highest wages you can afford. Constant turnover due to low wages can quickly increase your business costs and erode any savings realized initially. If necessary, stretch the company budget to pay a little more. Low pay can be a false economy in the long term.

■ Recognize and reward entry-level workers for their accomplishments. Again, "entry level" does not translate into "unimportant." Take time to acknowledge the worth of entry-level employees. Avoid, however, shallow or routine praise given simply because "that's what the book says to do." Employees, especially the older workers, quickly recognize this and it can do more harm than good.

■ Compliment employees according to their skill levels. An inexperienced employee may deserve and appreciate a compliment in a situation where an experienced employee would actually scoff at a compliment for something so routine. Tailor your praise (and criticism) to the person and his level of expertise.

■ Offer cash rewards on an ongoing basis. For someone on entry-level job wages, even small cash rewards on a regular basis can be important.

■ Award a 'personal day' for special achievements. Some workers may value and appreciate time off as much as cash.

■ Offer a choice of rewards. One employee may choose cash as a reward for achieving a goal; another employee may choose time off instead. Allow employees to choose what is important to them.

- Be flexible. Consider offering flexible working hours to employees. This may benefit the company as well as motivate your workers.

- Consider a combination of sick-vacation-personal days: the employee may be absent from work a certain number of days each year, whether for vacation, sick or personal. The number of days is the same but how the employee uses the days is up to him, no explanation required.

- Offer financial assistance for education as an incentive for entry-level workers to grow within the company. Consider tying the assistance to longevity with the company. An employee who uses the assistance may "pay off" the loan by remaining with the company for a pre-determined period of time.

- Have meals brought in occasionally. For example, on the last Friday of the month, give all employees a longer lunch break and have pizza delivered along with beverages.

- Listen to employees, and then respond—just listening is not enough. If the answer to a suggestion or request is "no," tell the employee and offer an explanation. Otherwise, employees feel management is only pretending to listen to their concerns. This can also happen if the answer is always "no."

- Take time to know your employees as individuals. An advantage for small business owners is they often have the opportunity to know employees on a more personal level and to have a better understanding of what motivates them as individuals.

IV

The Essentials of Great Customer Service

31

Make Your Customers Say "Wow!"

I travel a lot and spend a considerable amount of time at airports, renting cars and staying the night at hotels.

On one recent trip, I had a tight connection where I hoped and prayed my luggage would make it onto the plane. Well, guess what? No luggage. I was disappointed, but I expected it to happen.

My next move was to rent a car and start toward my client's location. At the terminal, I presented myself at the Enterprise car rental counter. Now, if you are like me, you have reached a point in your life where you just expect poor service. You expect to be treated like a robot, a sub-human or a clod of dirt. I soon found out this customer experience was going to be different.

The interaction began like you'd expect, some nameless guy asking for my credit card and driver's license. Then something unusual happened. The young man stood up, reached over the counter and shook my hand. It wasn't one of those dead fish kind of handshakes, but a real strong, glad-to-meet-you handshake. I almost fell out of my shoes in shock. Wow!

In my entire life, there has never been a car rental person stand up and shake my hand. Most people in other rental agencies could care less if I showed up or not. Well, this young man was amazing. He finished all the paperwork and asked me to sign those blank spaces on the contract; all the while I was trying to compose myself from the handshake experience. For all I know, I could have agreed to rent the car for $2,000 a day. But at that point I didn't care. I was beside myself.

Then he did it again. He stood up, walked around the counter and shook my hand one more time. Then he said, "Mr. Smith, we appreciate your business." I was blown away.

Here is an important fact to remember. A Gallup survey showed a customer who is "emotionally connected" to a place of business is likely to spend 46 percent more money there than a customer who is merely "satisfied" but not emotionally bonded.

Good customer service is expected, but customer loyalty is the goal. No matter what kind of business you manage, customer loyalty is critical. You don't want your customers to be merely "satisfied," you want them to be loyal—to be excited about your business. You want them to come back to you over and over again, not to your competition.

32

Great Customer Service is about Small Details

My family and I recently returned from a trip to Cabo San Lucas, Mexico. Traveling outside the United States gives reason for apprehension something might go wrong. Security delays, customs, the threat of terrorism or just the inconvenience of traveling makes vacationing more difficult than ever before. Often, what could be a great vacation is ruined by small details.

My wife handles all my travel and our family vacation arrangements. In this case, she used the Internet to plan our entire vacation, causing me even more concern something would go wrong.

As our plane circled the airport in Los Cabos, all I could see was one small landing strip among the cacti, sand and desert. My brain kicked into gear and began to analyze all the mistakes, bad service or disasters awaiting us.

To my surprise, transportation was standing by for us at the airport. The 45-minute trip to the resort was uneventful. The air conditioning in the van worked perfectly. The driver was courteous and helpful. So far, so good.

The arched gateway of La Hacienda Del Mar Beach Resort greeted our arrival. The doorman took our baggage and asked one profound question: "Would you like margaritas or lemonade?" After traveling on a plane for eight hours and 45 minutes, small details become magical.

If you own or manage a customer service business, the recipe for exceptional service boils down to the small details. Some of those details may be as simple as friendly employees, clean bathrooms or something that adds value to the customer experience. When designing your customer service plan, consider what small details you can provide making your place of business stand out in the hearts and minds of your customers. Consider the following:

■ I rarely visit art museums and galleries, but I was attracted to a small one near my hotel in San Francisco. This place was a treasure trove of paintings from both the living and the dead. There were originals by many of the masters, including my personal favorite, Norman Rockwell. In fact, one of my best loved works was right there in front of my eyes. I was thrilled with this place and so impressed I gave my business card to one of the people working there. As a result, I now get e-mails from this gallery every time they have a showing.

■ Most businesses lose 15 to 20 percent of their customers each year because they do not keep in touch. This gallery's e-mail marketing strategy provides an easy and inexpensive way to keep itself memorable. I only wish I had the money to purchase one of those pieces of art.

- The Lost Sock, a Laundromat in Richmond, Va., added a totally new dimension to the soapy floors and broken washers normally found in most Laundromats. Every Thursday night they have an "open mike" event. About 100 guests come to wash their laundry, have a few beers and watch their friends perform.

- A unique store located in Stone Mountain, Ga., specializes only in hot sauces and spices. They include a $2 bill with a little red pepper-shaped sticker applied to the back of the bill with the customer's change. The sticker has their store name and phone number. Since most people don't give out $2 bills, customers usually carry them in their wallets for a long time and show them to their friends. This bill and its accompanying sticker has become a marketing campaign for the business.

- The Jordan's Furniture stores located in Massachusetts sell more furniture per square foot than any other furniture store in the country. Everything from their zany television commercials, purple painted parking lots and the multimedia Motion Odyssey Movie ride, commonly known as M.O.M., helped to build a million-dollar industry. Loading dock employees occasionally dress in tuxedos. When shoppers drive around the back to pick up their furniture, they surprise them by washing their car windows, car tires and provide free hot dogs.

- One retail organization dramatically increased its sales and improved its level of customer service by allowing employees to design their customer service strategy. The owners wanted to design a more customer-focused, bottom-up, employee-driven store, where everyone could take ownership. The end result was a task force consisting of supervisors, managers and front-line employees who designed a pocket card with the "20 Commandments of Customer Service." Now each manager and employee carries this card with them at all times. The store is enjoying improved employee attitudes, reduced turnover and a rising level of customer service in the store.

The Customer Service Commandments are listed in the next chapter.

33
Customer Service Commandments

1. The vision statement will be known, owned and energized by all employees.

2. Our motto is: "We go beyond the call of duty." Help coworkers and practice cross-training to promote a positive work environment. All employees shall practice the three steps of service:

   A. Demonstrate a friendly and caring attitude.

   B. Anticipate and exceed customer needs and expectations.

   C. Offer your business card and express your desire to help them in the future.

4. All employees will successfully complete our training program to ensure they understand how to perform to the standards of their position.

5. Each employee will understand his work area and company goals.

6. All employees will know the needs of their customers and fellow employees so we may offer the products and

services they expect. Offer your business card to the customer.

7. Each employee shall regularly report defects throughout the store.

8. Any employee who receives a customer complaint "owns" the complaint.

9. Instant customer pacification will be ensured by all. React quickly to correct the problem immediately. Do everything you possibly can to never lose a customer.

10. The highest levels of cleanliness are the responsibility of every employee.

11. Treat every customer with respect and smile. We are on stage. Always make positive eye contact and use language like, "Good morning," "Certainly," "I'll be happy to," and "My pleasure."

12. Always speak well of your store in and out of the workplace.

13. Accompany a customer to the correct aisle instead of pointing to another area of the store.

14. Always use correct telephone etiquette. Answer the phone within three rings with a "smile" and avoid transfers when possible. If necessary, ask the customer, "May I place you on hold?" Be knowledgeable of store merchandise and equipment.

15. Uniforms are to be immaculate: Wear proper and safe footwear (clean and polished) and your correct nametag. Take pride in your personal appearance.

16. Notify your supervisor of any hazards, injuries, equipment or assistance that you need. Practice energy conservation and proper maintenance and repair of company property and equipment at all times.

17. It is every employee's responsibility to protect the assets of the store.

18. All employees are empowered to reward others for going beyond the call of duty.

19. All employees will be on time when reporting for their shift or returning from lunch or break.

20. Thou shalt carry the 20 commandments on thy person at all times when working.

34

Seven Steps that Build Customer Loyalty

Most businesses spend more time and energy trying to find new customers instead of retaining those they have. The logic behind customer retention is simple: It costs far less money to keep customers happy than to spend much more money recruiting new ones. Loyal customers tell their friends about your business and will spend more money than the new ones.

I dread eating at airports. If you travel as much as I do, you are probably familiar with the "3 B's" as it applies to airport fare: bad food, bad attitudes, bad timing.

I had an early flight to catch at the Ontario, Calif., airport recently. I found myself standing outside the closed and gated doorway to an Applebee's restaurant 10 minutes before its official opening time. I just knew they would be late and expected to receive the usual grumpy service common at most airports the world over. I was wrong!

Bam! The clock struck 5, the lights popped on and this charming lady opened the doors. She greeted me with a smile, a warm "hello" and told me to sit anywhere I wanted. I never had seen such a positive attitude at 5 o'clock in the morning.

For the next hour, I watched Felicia cheerfully greet customers, many of whom she called by name. They were the "regulars," she said. Felicia was the remarkable person who made that small restaurant pleasant and memorable. Next time I return to the Ontario Airport, I guarantee this is the restaurant I am going to first.

Here are seven steps to build customer loyalty.

1. Select the right people.

In the book, "From Good to Great," Jim Collins said, "People are not your most important asset, the right people are." Most businesses do a poor job of hiring people. They hire just anyone and place them on the front-line with customers. Spend more time recruiting and hiring the right people with good personalities. Focus on those who are friendly and demonstrate an interest and enthusiasm for the job. Consider using personality profiles as part of the hiring process. These profiles help identify true personality characteristics of your applicants.

2. Sensationalize the experience for your customers.

Good service is not good enough. A Gallup survey showed a customer who is "emotionally connected" to your place of business is likely to spend 46 percent more money there than a customer who is merely "satisfied" but not emotionally bonded.

3. Set performance standards.

Outline specific steps how employees are to act, speak and respond to customer needs and requests. If you let your employees decide how to act, there is no telling what they will do. One of our clients developed 20 customer service commandments to outline the specific actions they wanted their service people to demonstrate. Each day a supervisor conducts a 10-minute review of one of the commandments with his employees.

4. Sustain ongoing training and reinforcement.

Most people are not born with great customer service skills. Effective customer service training must be reinforced and taught on a recurring basis. For example, the Ritz-Carlton Hotels provide a thorough customer service training program for all of its employees during their employee orientation program. Then each supervisor conducts a daily "line-up" 10 minutes before each shift to review one of their twenty customer service commandments with his employees.

5. Specify incentives for good behavior.

Yes, employees want to be paid well, but they also want to be treated with respect and shown appreciation. The front-line supervisor has the greatest impact on motivating and retaining employees. Reward those who exceed the standards and provide development for those who do not.

6. Survey your customers.

On average, businesses lose 15 to 20 percent of their customers each year. If your organization has $10 million in sales, that represents a $2 million loss every year. All businesses encounter this defection rate, but few do anything to improve it. One company sends out a customer service report card to its top customers every month. They ask them for an evaluation on four specific criteria. Then they tabulate the results and publicly display them for all employees to see. This process helps to improve customer satisfaction, build loyalty and increase sales as well.

7. Seek customer complaints with enthusiasm.
For every complaint you receive there are at least 10 other customers that have the same criticism. A portion of those 10 people just took their business to your competitor. Look at customer complaints as an opportunity for improvement.

35

Front-Line Customer Focus Improves the Bottom-Line

The Blue Willow Inn is one hour east of Atlanta in Social Circle, Ga. A few years ago, some friends of mine decided to stop at this antebellum restaurant they had heard so much about. Food was already on their table when they overheard Vivian, their server, tell guests at another table she was sorry that they didn't accept credit cards.

My friends panicked when they realized they might not have enough cash to pay for their meal. They asked Vivian to come over to their table and repeat what she had just said. She confirmed the fact that, no, they didn't accept credit cards; but Vivian quickly countered with this statement. "Don't let that ruin your meal. You see I have my own money and I will pay for your meal." She then opened her purse and she showed them her cash. My friends were in shock and couldn't believe what they just heard. The server was going to pay for their meal! They will never forget Vivian or the Blue Willow Inn.

Louis Van Dyke, the owner of the Blue Willow Inn, says this customer-oriented attitude is common among his entire staff. His vision of a customer-oriented restaurant has empowered

his staff to become innovative in their approach with customers. The results speak for themselves. Since 1985, his business
has tripled. Over half of his customers travel an hour or more
to eat there. The Blue Willow Inn does very little advertising
because most of its business comes from word of mouth.

The loyalty of Van Dyke's customers is phenomenal. They
now accept credit cards. However, he recalls in previous years
there were only 15 to 20 people who didn't have enough cash
to pay for their meals. So each of those people were given a
courtesy check to take home with them and asked to mail a
check back. Remarkably, everyone mailed the money back.

36

The Battleground for Good Customer Service

At the front entrance of Stu Leonard's Dairy Store stands a large boulder. Engraved on the boulder are these words:

"Our Policy

Rule 1: The customer is always right!
Rule 2: If the customer is ever wrong, re-read rule 1."

This inscription in stone illustrates the attitude needed for successful customer service in this highly competitive market we live in today. Stu Leonard has successfully transformed this policy into profitable action to over 100,000 weekly customers. Leonard's reputation for exceptional customer service has gained international recognition.

The next decade will be a battleground with few winners. It will be a time of intense competition and the champions will be the ones who know exactly what they are doing.

The primary competitive advantage of this century is the speed with which you meet your customers' needs. The recipe for exceptional customer service boils down to a few basic ingredients: flexibility, friendliness, price and exceeding your customers' needs and expectations— lots of little things that make a tremendous difference.

If you are going to survive as a customer-driven business, you are going to have to provide unequaled customer service—no exceptions. Right or wrong, the customer is always right. The result will be greater satisfaction for both workers and customers and an exceptional bottom line. Here are some key points to keep in mind.

- Build a long-term relationship with your customers, not a one-night stand. Call your customers on the telephone or stand at the door as they are leaving. Ask them how they were treated, what you could have done better. Will they return to buy something else?

- Pretend you are the customer and evaluate your own business. Use a telephone and call your business. How long does it take to get an answer? How are you handled? Do they use your first name? Did they make you feel welcome or were you treated like a nuisance?

- Measure what's important to your customers. The customer decides what exceptional service is, not management. Identify what they need and expect, and develop a system to show how well you are doing in each area that is important to them.

- Use the Internet. Can you provide sales, service or information on the Internet? More and more people are using the Web for everything from fine wines to contact lenses.

- Build loyal employees. The front-line person is the most important individual in your organization. Treat him better than you treat your customers. We all know how difficult it is to find and keep good workers. If they feel management cares about them, they will reflect the same respect to your customers.

- Use "hero awards." Make heroes out of your customer service people and allow co-workers to reward each other for doing a good job.

- Provide a customer service guarantee that excites people. Customers are sick of loopholes and limited warranties. People are tired of hassles and long lines and forms to fill out. Sure, there will be people who will take advantage of you, but the trade off is a lot more people will buy, visit, tell their friends about and spend their money with you and not your competitor.

- Don't stop. Continuously improve all areas relating to customer service. The competition never stops, neither should you. Evaluate and visit other good businesses and see what they are doing.

37

Case Study: Singapore Airlines

It was the food cart bashing my knee that woke me from a pleasant dream. As I grabbed my knee, I saw the flight attendant with the "hit-and-run" food cart heading down the aisle.

I was on the final leg of a long trip, flying on a well-known but mediocre domestic airline once known for its good service. Only hours before, I was traveling on Singapore Airlines (SIA). SIA is so superior it leaves other carriers in its vapor trails—even other overseas carriers known for great service. The positive experience on SIA makes the Air Passengers' Bill of Rights completely unnecessary.

How does it create this experience? It places the needs of passengers first and offers service that is above and beyond the ordinary. Even in economy class, the experience is unforgettable. Pillows and blankets are carefully placed on every seat. Once in the air, smiling attendants offer champagne or orange juice. Passengers receive an attractive kit containing a toothbrush, toothpaste and socks for the trip. At the beginning and the end of each flight, passengers receive hot towels to freshen up.

All classes enjoy first-class treatment. I don't think I ever saw a peanut on this flight. Passengers are presented with a menu with choices. The food in the back of the plane is better than other carriers' first-class flights. After meals, attendants bring liqueurs, beer, juice or anything else you want—at no charge. I almost wanted to say, "Leave me alone—quit feeding me!"

Singapore Airlines can delight its customers with high-level service because it hires and supports workers who like providing service and who feel aligned with the company's overall goals. Here are the important factors contributing to SIA great customer experience.

Staff training and development.
SIA's significant investment in staff development and training—conducted in good times and bad—enables staff members to stay focused and continuously upgrade their performance. Training and development fights complacency and keeps crew members capable of handling demanding situations. It also gives the airline a distinct advantage. First, it demonstrates that continuous learning and development help people do a better job, which in turn helps individuals improve their potential. Second, it allows SIA to stay ahead of its competition while other carriers may be cutting back.

No fear of change and innovation.
SIA is known for innovation. Instead of copying other airlines, it takes the lead. Instead of charging passengers a $5 "entertainment fee," it gives away headsets. Instead of charging for drinks, it gives them away—along with free postcards and the postage needed to mail them. Passengers in

the "Raffles Class" section have seats that recline into beds. SIA benchmarks other service industries such as hotels and restaurants to make its service more comfortable, convenient and creative.

Consistent communication.

With over 27,000 staff members representing 25 nationalities, communication is critical. SIA keeps staff informed of important matters through newsletters and publications, regular meetings between management and staff, and a Staff Ideas in Action program that helps move forward new suggestions and ideas for action and improvement.

Recognize, reinforce and reward the right behavior.

Excellent service is a learned behavior that requires constant reinforcement and recognition. Unless an organization develops systems and processes to reward and recognize the behavior it needs for success, it will never get it. SIA rewards excellent performance with increased pay and promotions, but reserves its most prestigious award for superior acts of customer service. The Deputy Chairman's Award is provided each year to people who have managed customer situations with selfless acts of service. It is a badge of honor coveted by all employees. Winners and their families fly to Singapore for a special dinner. Information about winners and their families is published in the monthly Outlook magazine.

Customers always come first.

Customer service directs and guides SIA in all it does. SIA places a priority on quality service. All questions are answered and decisions made based on the needs of the customer. While other airlines cut back on service to make more profits, SIA retains the customers' needs as first priority. The bottom line for SIA is not the plane, the seat or the destination. The bottom line is delivering exceptional service and personifying that service.

38

Customer Service
the Ritz-Carlton Way

Customer service seems to be headed in the same direction as the Titanic. Why? One reason is most Americans feel customer service jobs are beneath them and of little importance. Secondly, many organizations have eliminated the human element, replacing it with a lower-cost, impersonal conglomeration of voice mail, e-mail, and online request forms. For many shortsighted service companies, it is about cutting costs, cutting corners and driving up profits.

The Ritz-Carlton Hotels make customer service an art form. Unlike other places, they know if you treat your customers well and make a special effort to please them, guess what? They come back, tell their friends and maintain a long lasting relationship of loyalty.

My wife and I recently stayed at the Reynolds Plantation Ritz-Carlton at Lake Oconee, Ga. Upon checking in, we dropped off our bags and took a seat in the lobby to enjoy the view of the lake. A few minutes later a service person named Susan introduced herself and began a friendly conversation. She asked us why we were staying at the hotel. I said, "We are here for our wedding anniversary." With a very big smile she told us,

"Congratulations. Let me get you some champagne." Wow! This was the first of two episodes at this hotel that would capture my loyalty as a guest of Ritz-Carlton.

Later that evening a knock at the door caught us by surprise. Greeting us again was Susan. This time she surprised us with a luscious piece of cake carefully presented on a plate. In icing was this inscription, "Happy Anniversary."

It was not a stroke of luck we stumbled across Susan. She, as well as other Ritz-Carlton employees, are carefully selected and thoroughly trained in how to identify guests' unspoken requests. They follow a process called the "Three Steps of Service."

Step 1: Warm welcome

Step 2: Anticipation and compliance

Step 3: Fond farewell

It is during Step 2 where staff members seek out and discover guests' needs or wishes. Then they present it in a way to create a "moment of truth." In our case, it was the champagne and the anniversary cake.

Now, let me make an important point to the critics. I know many of you are saying, "I expect to be treated well at fine hotels—it is what I pay for." Let's consider this. The same principles and standards of behavior demonstrated at the Ritz-

Carlton can also be applied at your local car dealership, bank or any business, can't they?

Just imagine going to your car repair shop with your car. Within 60 minutes they fix it right the first time and deliver it to your door cleaner than when you dropped it off. How many people would you tell about it? Surely, the proprietor of the car repair shop would see exponential growth. The additional profits and the revenue would outweigh the added time and expense spent exceeding their customers' expectations.

In today's competitive economy, business leaders have to make a choice. They can choose to be average or they can choose to become exceptional. It almost goes without saying, but it is easier and less expensive to be average. Which choice will you make?

V

Manage for Top Performance

39

How To Attract, Retain and Motivate Today's Workforce

Business leaders should realize creating a workplace that attracts, retains and engages their workforce is important no matter the state of the economy. The key point to remember is talented and skilled people are always in demand. The more skill and talent they possess, the more likely they can leave you for another employer. Employers should not only be concerned about retaining the employees they have, but should also focus on creating an environment that makes them as productive as possible.

During the last economic downturn, many employers took a short-term approach to managing the people side of their businesses. They cut back and downsized so severely that it forced those who remained to work two or more jobs. So when the economy recovered, many of those alienated employees jumped ship just when their employer needed them the most. These actions can damage morale, which could prevent you from attracting new talent and retaining the good ones you have.

Provide a Positive Working Environment

Senior leaders who take personal responsibility for retention in their organizations have lower turnover and higher productivity than those that do not. Jim Goodnight is the co-founder and president of SAS in Raleigh-Durham, N.C. SAS is the largest software development companies in the United States. Its progressive work environment and host of family-friendly benefits keep the company's turnover rate far below the national average. Goodnight said, "My assets leave work for home at 5 o'clock or later each night. It is my job to bring them back each day." Wise executives realize the responsibility for creating a positive work environment cannot be delegated. It starts at the top.

Recognize, Reinforce and Reward

Money and benefits are important factors in attracting and retaining people, but reward and recognition help meet that basic human need to feel appreciated and rewarded for what one does. A successful reward and recognition program does not have to be complicated or involve money to be effective.

Disney World views reward and recognition as key parts of the compensation package. An extensive program helps create a supportive environment, contributes to employee retention and encourages employee engagement. They have over 20 different recognition programs such as "Applause-O-Gram" cards and "Thumbs Up" gift certificates provided to individuals. Additionally, each department has custom-designed reward programs providing on-the-spot recognition. New employees are asked to participate in their own reward strategy by listing in their file the things they would like to be rewarded with; for example, time off, movie tickets or public recognition. The highest form of public recognition is when top-performing employees have their names stenciled on the storefronts along "Main Street."

Graham Weston, co-founder and CEO of Rackspace Hosting, gives the keys to his BMW M3 convertible to his top-performing employees for a week. This creative way to reward employees has a bigger impact than cash. He says, "If you gave somebody a $200 bonus, it wouldn't mean very much. When someone gets to drive my car for a week, they never forget it."

Involve and Engage the Workforce
People may show up for work, but are they engaged and productive? Individuals are more committed and engaged when there is a process for them to contribute their ideas and suggestions. This gives them a sense of ownership.

The Sony Corporation fosters the exchange of ideas within departments by sponsoring an annual Idea Exposition. During the exposition, scientists and engineers display projects and ideas they are developing. Open only to Sony's employees, this process creates a healthy climate of innovation and engages all those who participate.

Develop the Potential of Individuals
Many people rate educational and training opportunities as being just as important as the money they make. In a study by Linkage Inc., more than 40 percent of the respondents said they would consider leaving their present employer for

another job with the same benefits if that job provided better career development and greater challenges.

Deloitte is listed as one of the "Top 100 Best Places to Work." The company discovered several years ago it was losing talented people to other companies. Executives conducted exit surveys and found 70 percent of those employees who left to take new jobs and careers outside the company could have found the same jobs and careers within Deloitte.

As a result they created Deloitte Career Connections, an intranet-based development and career coaching program for all employees. During the first week of implementation, over 2,000 employees took advantage of the program.

Not only does the program provide new job and mentoring opportunities, but Career Connections offers a host of career development tools such as self-assessments, tools to develop resumes and articles on various job-seeking strategies within the company.

Evaluate and Improve Continuously

Someone said, "If you don't know where you are going, any road will lead you there." The evaluation and improvement process must include important indicators such as turnover, employee attitudes and how well managers are taking care of employees.

Here is a checklist of items that should be included in your process.

- Conduct exit interviews on the real reasons people leave your organization.

■ Ask employees who have been with your business longer than five years why they stay with you.

■ Ask new employees what attracted them to your business.

■ Evaluate which departments have better or worse retention rates than others.

■ Create a retention plan for those key individuals who have the greatest impact on profitability and productivity.

40
The Quest for the Best

Performance management is about creating an environment where people know what is expected of them, have access to the tools they need for their work, and are supported in their quest to do their best. It's about creating people who feel good about themselves and their accomplishments, who in turn will reward the organization with loyalty and high retention. Performance management has three key goals:

1. Creating a workplace where top performers want to stay;

2. Transforming people who are not "stars" into top performers; and

3. Aligning behavior and actions toward the goals of the business enterprise.

Aligning behavior and actions with your business's goals is the bottom line for staying in business. You need to define and then create the behaviors needed for maximum efficiency and productivity.

People tell me the work ethic is declining. They say new employees don't show up and skip shifts when they please. In effect, they are saying, "these people are flawed and there's nothing I can do about it."

As I've stressed throughout my books and articles, there is plenty that leaders can do to turn an average or even a poor performer into a highly productive one. Leaders have something called "discretionary effort." Basically, discretionary effort is what they can do to create superior performance. It is situational and varies depending on the individual and circumstance.

To effectively manage performance, you must first determine what "high performance" means and how to structure an environment to elicit it. When this spadework is finished, it's easy to design programs and actions that reinforce performance at the back end.

But be careful. Performance management is not manipulation. People never respond well to control or manipulation, and will flee an environment in which these strategies are dressed up as "performance management." Consider these performance management programs:

Lottery System
One company uses a lottery system to reduce absenteeism by 75 percent and costs by 62 percent. Only employees with no absenteeism during the month can participate; prizes include a television, a bicycle and so on.

Perfect Attendance Program
One large rental business encourages attendance by giving employees with perfect attendance during the year $300, a limousine ride to a restaurant for a free dinner with their spouses and a gift certificate worth $100. Employees of a county government receive perfect attendance certificates for

not missing a day of work during the month. This successful program made a significant improvement in the absenteeism level among employees. It was so successful, in fact, that some employees weren't keeping doctor appointments because it would make them ineligible for the monthly award. The county recognized the unavoidable need to occasionally have appointments during the business day and instituted a second award for people who miss less than eight hours a month. This allowed employees to go to the doctor and still gave an incentive for them to take a few hours off rather than the entire day.

Service Over and Above Requirements (SOAR)

At Nationwide Mutual Insurance Company, customers, managers and peers nominate employees for "service over and above." Regional six-member boards (all volunteers) meet weekly or monthly to review the nominations and select a winner. The winner chooses a prize from a catalog that includes magnets, pins, mugs, writing pens and sweatshirts.

Greased Monkey Award

At one organization managers present a "Greased Monkey Award" to the computer technician who is best at resolving problems with computer programs. They are awarded with a plastic toy monkey in a jar of Vaseline along with a $50 dinner certificate.

41

Low-Access Versus High-Access Organizations

There are two basic types of organizations: low-access and high-access. Good communication is a hallmark of a good work environment. At its heart, communication is all about access.

In a low-access organization, the flow of communication is guarded and restricted—constipated, in fact. People find themselves kept in the dark, like mushrooms, stuffed in narrow confines based on job descriptions, ranking and where they sit on the organizational chart. It's no surprise that low-access organizations—many of them hierarchical—have greater difficulty responding to change, fluctuating customer needs and the fluidity of the modern workplace.

In contrast, a high-access organization thrives on information and shares it to the maximum extent possible. The more information people have, the more quickly they can respond to the changing needs of customers and the environment. High-access companies are committed to open communication.

Symptoms of the low-access organization

It's a regulatory-based culture, rather than a people-based. A low-access organization is structured around rules, regulations and policies. Management places more emphasis on enforcing rules than eliminating unnecessary rules and regulations.

Decision-making is centralized. The low-access organization has a top-down decision-making process.

Mistakes are hard to fix. The low-access organization places little emphasis on innovation and fixing deficiencies. Because only the people on top of the organization are responsible for interpreting and approving any changes to regulations, decision-making slows down because the responsibility and power to make decisions is taken away from those who need it the most.

Change is resisted. A low-access organization protects itself from change. Only a disaster, a threat or a public relations crisis is enough to initiate change. In the compartmentalized, functionally aligned, department-by-department organization, there is an expert for everything.

The organizational structure is rigid and inflexible. In its worst form, a low-access organization becomes a caste system. Top-down layering dictates what roles to take, to whom to talk, and with whom to associate. Rank, position and educational degrees become more important than results.

42

In God We Trust, All Others Bring Data

The head of Electro Scientific Industries once said, "Trust is the grease that keeps an organization going." Trust is a key factor needed for effective leadership.

Leadership and trust go hand-in-hand. Whether you are a minister or a corporate CEO, you cannot expect people to trust you—you have to earn it first. We have become skeptical and callous.

Furthermore, maintaining trust is like walking on eggs—slow going and easily crushed. Many executives unintentionally damage their credibility and trust. Here are some ways to maintain a high trust level within your organization.

Your personal life is your public life.
Your personal life reflects who you really are. If you are in a leadership position, your personal life is open to scrutiny. Your ability to lead others will increase if people respect you. You may not like it, but that is the way it is.

Do what you say you will do.

How many times has someone told you, "I'll get back to you on that," but never followed up? Don't make promises you can't or won't keep. Trust breaks down when promises are broken.

Tell the truth.

The worst thing you can do is to not be open and honest with people. Trying to hide information will always catch up with you. Tell people everything they need to know, even if it's bad news. It's better to say too much than too little.

Treat everyone with respect.

You may not like everyone you work with, but you must treat them as if you do. People want to feel they have value and worth as individuals. Give everyone a chance to improve and attempt to understand and place their interests in proper priority.

Show appreciation.

Surprise your employees by doing something unexpected for them. When you see one of your workers doing something good, write a note of appreciation or walk up and just tell them. They will appreciate you and trust you more.

Avoid favoritism.

Don't turn to the same person for help over and over again. Train and develop all your employees so everyone has equal opportunity to prove himself and the workload is shared equally. Ensure minorities are fairly represented at all levels of the organization and provided the same opportunity for advancement.

Consistently enforce the rules.

Eliminate unnecessary rules, regulations and policies, and enforce all the rest. When you selectively enforce policies, mistrust increases. No matter how clear the rules seem to you, everyone has a different perception. What appears unnecessary to you is important to someone else. Either enforce it or eliminate it.

Treat people as equals.

Because of many corporate scandals, more pressure is placed on boards and executives to give all employees the same privileges normally reserved for executives. If executives can sell their stock options, why can't other employees? Privileges and perks will be under greater scrutiny by both the media and rank and file.

Don't tell jokes at others' expense.

Telling jokes is a good way to lower your trust quotient. The most harmless joke will offend someone. Even Dilbert cartoons damage the credibility and trustworthiness of management. They create a perception that all managers are stupid.

43

Having Fun at Work Engages and Energizes the Workforce

Studies show businesses that engage and energize their workforce are more productive and have higher retention rates. Every now and then you should break up the normal routine and do something different. A once-a-year trip to the mountains, birthday celebrations, or something silly like having a "crazy hat day," can go a long way to make a big difference. Small, informal celebrations are many times more effective than a once-a-year formal event. Here are a few examples of simple but powerful ideas and tips used by different organizations to energize their workforce.

Man Overboard Award

CIGNA believes in rewarding employees who go above and beyond for their customers. The Overboard Award is a life-saving ring, which the president presents to an employee at a special ceremony. CIGNA also pays teams for implemented ideas that improve productivity with awards as high as $25,000.

Choose Your Own Reward

The owner of Miami-based Creative Staffing rewards her employees with parties, expensive dinners, chauffeured shopping sprees, spa sessions and cooking lessons with Paul Prudhomme. She lets her employees decide what they want, then figures how much the package costs and also how much additional business they have to generate to cover those costs. Choose your own reward—sounds like fun!

Engineering Bucks

The technicians at The Weather Channel in Atlanta created their own recognition system called Tech Bucks. All they did was photocopy a one-dollar bill and give five of them out at the beginning of each month. They give them to each other for doing a good job. At the end of the month they tally up who has the most and the winner gets a special prize.

Humor Corner

One company decided to improve its work environment by creating a humor corner. They picked the area around their fax machine where they began posting cartoons, illustrations and other items designed to relieve stress. At the end of each week a prize was awarded for the best submission.

The Extra Mile

United Services Automobile Association (USAA) provided blank thank-you note stationery for its workers called The Extra Mile. Employees are encouraged to say "Thank you" to each other for the help they receive at work. The most surprising thing happened on the first day USAA printed the notes—they ran out! The company couldn't keep up with the demand.

Fat Friday

Just about everybody loves to eat. The first Friday of each month is celebration time at Texas A&M University. Everyone brings food to share and they celebrate birthdays for the month as well as work anniversaries.

Surprise celebrations

Often it's the unexpected and informal gestures that employees enjoy as much as formal awards. Conduct frequent, unannounced recognition and award celebrations, such as a pizza party. If you don't have a reason to hold a get-together for the workforce, invent one.

Having fun

Hal Rosenbluth is the CEO of Rosenbluth International Inc., one of the nation's largest travel services companies. He believes in creating a fun work environment. He starts by hiring "nice people" since he believes nice people like to work together and have fun. Officers dedicate every Tuesday afternoon to serving high tea and discussing corporate values and other matters of importance to new recruits at the company's Philadelphia headquarters. A toll-free 800 number is available for any associate to contact Rosenbluth. He uses a sort of Crayola-Rorschach test by sending associates crayons and blank paper to render their view of the company. A "happiness barometer" team meets every six months to benchmark attitudes and enjoyment levels.

Faux Pas Award

Sometimes it's fun to recognize an employee's goof. A plaque is passed around the organization at a monthly social event with the current recipient's name engraved. The "keeper" of the award is responsible for selecting the next deserving recipient.

After-dinner phone call

Even though you took time during the workday to thank the employee who went "above and beyond," go a step further and call them at home after dinner to say thanks. You might be surprised how much this can mean to people.

Breakfast with the President

The Human Resources Department of Nations Healthcare Inc. initiated a "Breakfast with the President" program to improve communications between employees and the CEO. Each breakfast begins at approximately 8:15 a.m., with coffee and biscuits served by the staff, and ends when the discussion ends. As a result, they generated higher morale and a sense of open communication.

Fun Fridays

A Dallas, Texas, unit of Sprint Corporation uses "Fun Fridays" to energize workers. Themes have included exchanging a plant with a co-worker and ice cream socials where managers wear aprons and serve sundaes.

Peat and Feet

Warehouse employees of Lantana Peat and Soil, a subsidiary of Coventry Industries Corporation in Boca Raton,

Fla., spend many hours on their feet as they move peat moss used on Christmas plants. Robert Hausman, chairman of Coventry, rewards their long hours with a free visit to a podiatrist.

Bowling with Turkeys

Hotel tradition calls for employees at the Hyatt Regency in Lexington, Ky., to wrap a 12-pound frozen turkey with electrical tape then roll it 50 feet down the loading dock and try to turn over as many wine bottle "bowling pins" as possible. Winners get a pumpkin pie.

44

Everyone is Talking, But No One is Communicating

Today's businesses must change course quickly. Communication and information are essential to innovation, good customer service, high retention and change. And it has to flow freely.

In a survey conducted by Chart Your Course International, respondents were asked the question, "To improve your workplace environment what would you like to see your executives/supervisors/managers do?"

Sixty-nine percent of the respondents said, "Be better at communicating."

You'd think with so many ways to communicate—cell phones, Internet, e-mail, personal digital assistants, pagers, etc—our ability to communicate would improve. But the opposite seems to be true: as technology advances, the quality of communication declines. As the quantity of communication tools increases, the quality of communication decreases.

In 1995, the Boeing Company suffered its second-longest walkout ever when the Machinists Union led a 69-day strike against the company. Boeing lost hundreds of millions of dollars and experienced big customer service headaches when the company missed the delivery dates on 36 airliners.

Part of the problem was while Boeing preached teamwork and productivity, it sent jobs out to lower-cost subcontractors. The disconnect between what management was saying and what it was doing escalated tensions between the union and management.

Boeing's chairman and president blamed the strike on its "own lack of understanding of worker sentiment and on a failure to communicate corporate concerns to the workforce." He noted part of the problem lay with Boeing's "inability to communicate effectively on what we were about and why we were about it."

In 1998 UPS experienced a similar fate when its employees went on strike. UPS lost over $700 million in revenues and suffered a blow to its credibility and trust among its loyal employees. Speaking in retrospect, the Atlanta-based human resources director, said, "No one won." He noted the walkout could have been prevented if UPS had done a better job of communication prior to and during the negotiations.

UPS learned two important lessons from the strike. First, the employees did not fully understand their benefit packages prior to the strike. If they had understood them, much of the confusion could have been eliminated. The final settlement between the union and management did not significantly increase benefits over the previous contract.

Second, UPS underestimated the need to communicate during the actual negotiation process. To avoid confusing people during the rapidly shifting negotiations, it kept a tight rein on information—a major mistake, as it turned out. Employees wanted to know what was going on, and because they couldn't, many loyal employees felt betrayed by management and walked off the job. The lack of information created a backlash and anger, resentment, legal actions and lost revenues.

Finally, UPS learned never to assume people know what you think they know. When in doubt, over-communicate.

45
Using 360-Degree Feedback to Improve Performance

"Mirror, mirror on the wall, who is the fairest of them all?" Are you curious how others perceive your performance? Do you wonder how effective you are at what you do? Unfortunately, most people cannot accurately evaluate their performance. Perception is reality.

The 360-degree performance appraisal has gained popularity as a tool to accurately measure performance. In this down-sized economy executives are concerned how individual performance affects organizational performance, productivity and the bottom line.

Typical performance feedback methods are unreliable. As individuals, we receive feedback from two groups. On one extreme we hear from people who like us; on the other end of the spectrum, we hear from people who despise us. As long as we surround ourselves with "yes" people, we will never know what needs improving. Neither group is entirely accurate in its appraisal. The silent majority, the group in the middle, has the most valuable and valid feedback.

Most people compare the traditional performance appraisal process to standing on a broken bathroom scale that provides everyone the exact same weight. The annual, one-on-one performance appraisal provides biased and limited feedback. Personal chemistry plays a large part in evaluations. Studies show individuals who look like, act like and think like the boss will usually receive a better evaluation than individuals who are different. In more cases, supervisors avoid saying anything negative, fail to address shortcomings and lump everyone in the same middle-of-the-road performance scale.

The 360-degree assessment is a powerful tool for helping individuals improve, grow and develop their leadership skills. I worked with one individual who received excellent scores from her supervisor and board members. She "walked on water," one of them said. However, when I completed a 360-degree assessment, four out of five direct reports identified major weaknesses. She was a micromanager, over-controlling, and intimidated those who worked for her. The end result was a group of people afraid to take initiative and limited by her controlling management style. When she saw the report, she was willing to change her behavior and resolve the issues. If she had depended only on the feedback from her supervisor, she would have been oblivious to the problem.

The supervisor is only one person out of many possessing valuable input to the performance of the rated individual. Getting accurate feedback from all the groups of people we work with is more valuable than feedback from just one person. This assessment gathers information from people about an individual's performance as seen by the standards and expectations of his boss, himself, his peers, his direct reports and customers.

The development of effective skills begins with the awareness of ineffective behaviors. A 360-degree feedback assessment shows you what others think of your performance versus what it should be. By understanding the perception of others, you can improve.

How does it work?

The rated employee and his boss pick a group of eight to 12 individuals who have worked with the employee for a minimum of 90 days. The group should consist of stakeholders, including customers, direct reports, peers and the individual's direct supervisor. Most 360-degree assessments are conducted on a secure Web page consisting of 40 to 60 questions. At the conclusion, the rated employee receives a written report that includes the aggregate scores broken down by groups (supervisor, self, peers, direct reports, etc.).

These 360-degree assessments must be used with foresight and forethought. Critics say they are nothing more than popularity contests. Our organization has conducted dozens of assessments and found the input is much more fair and objective than other performance appraisals. In some cases, written comments provided by the stakeholders are the most helpful part of the process.

The 360-degree assessment points out blind spots individuals, team members and managers cannot see about themselves. Depending on the maturity level of the individual, this revelation can come as a blessing or a curse. Assessment results should be facilitated in a way that leads to a complete process of improvement. Follow-up and action plans for improvement are a critical part of this process.

46
Resolving Workplace Conflict

Conflict in the workplace is a painful reality and a key reason for poor productivity and frustration. Do you have people in your workplace that cause problems for everyone else? Do they create additional work for others? One point is clear: conflict does not magically go away and only gets worse when ignored.

Certain types of workplace conflict are readily identified. Other forms may not be so easily detected. Small, irritating events such as negative attitudes occur repeatedly over time and can cause people to strike out at each other. In many cases, conflict occurs at the senior level of the organization. In these situations some kind of intervention is needed.

What type of workplace conflict requires intervention? Anything that disrupts the office, impacts on productivity or poses a threat to other employees needs addressing. The degree to which you tolerate a situation before intervention may vary. A manager may not feel it necessary to intervene when a minor exchange of words occurs between employees—unless such an incident becomes a daily occurrence and expands beyond the employees initially involved. However, a situation where one employee threatens another requires immediate action.

When handling conflict, some basic guidelines apply.

Understand the situation.
Few situations are exactly as they seem or as presented to you by others. Before you try to settle the conflict, ensure you have investigated both sides of the issue.

Acknowledge the problem.
I remember an exchange between two board members. One member was frustrated with the direction the organization was taking. He told the other, "Just don't worry about it. It isn't that important." Keep in mind what appears to be a small issue to you can be a major issue with another. Acknowledging the frustration and concern is an important step in resolving the conflict.

Be patient and take your time.
The old adage, "haste makes waste," has more truth in it than we sometimes realize. Take time to evaluate all information. A too-quick decision does more harm than good when it turns out to be the wrong decision and further alienates the individual involved.

Avoid using coercion and intimidation.
Engaging in emotional outbursts or coercing people may stop the problem temporarily, but do not fool yourself into thinking it is a long-term solution. Odds are the problem will resurface. At that point not only will you have the ini-

tial problem to handle, but also the angry feelings that have festered below the surface during the interim.

Focus on the problem, not the individual.

Most people have known at least one problematic individual during their work experience. Avoid your own preconceived attitudes about individuals. Person X may not be the most congenial individual or he may just have a personality conflict with someone on your staff. This does not mean he does not have a legitimate problem or issue. Focus on identifying and resolving the conflict. If, after careful and thorough analysis, you determine the individual is the problem, then focus on the individual at that point.

Establish guidelines.

Before conducting a formal meeting between individuals, get both parties to agree to a few meeting guidelines. Ask them to express themselves calmly, as unemotionally as possible. Have them agree to attempt to understand each other's perspective. Tell them if they violate the guidelines the meeting will come to an end.

Keep the communication open.

The ultimate goal in conflict resolution is for both parties to resolve the issue between themselves. Allow both parties to express their viewpoint, but also share your perspective. Attempt to facilitate the meeting and help them pinpoint the real issue causing conflict.

Act decisively.
Once you have taken time to gather information, talked to all the parties involved and reviewed all the circumstances, make your decision and act. Don't leave the issue in limbo. Taking too long to make a decision could damage your credibility and their perception of you. They may view you as either too weak, too uncaring— or both—to handle the problem. Not everyone will agree with your decision, but at least they will know where you stand.

47

Total Quality Management According to Dr. W. Edwards Deming

I have read, studied and observed hundreds of management fads, management philosophies and management gurus during my lifetime. I am old enough to remember the 1970s and 80s when this country faced a worse economic condition than we are in today. At the same time, America was reeling from the competitive onslaught better made but less expensive products coming across the seas from Japan. This crisis triggered a reaction forcing a revolutionary change in how this country conducts business.

Few management philosophies have had a wider influence on the business world than quality management. It had one goal to tap the potential, abilities, skills and knowledge of the workforce. Furthermore, its goal was to systemize every aspect of the organization forcing a laser-like focus on exceptional customer satisfaction. The quality revolution claimed many names such as Total Quality Management (TQM) and Continuous Quality Improvement (CQI).

The most widely known quality expert at the time was Dr. W. Edwards Deming. At the end of World War II, Deming worked for the U.S. government and traveled to Japan to help rebuild their economy with his unique style of management. For years, Dr. Deming was more widely known in Japan than in his own country. His rise to iconic status in 1980 was attributed to Clare Crawford-Mason, a veteran news reporter and television producer, who produced a documentary for NBC on the decline of American competitiveness called, "If Japan Can ...Why Can't We?" The rest is history.

The key characteristics forming the foundation of the quality management philosophy are listed as follows:

Customer-driven focus
Place the customer as the center of the universe. Businesses strive to meet and exceed the customer's needs and expectations.

Continuous improvement
Demand continual improvement in all areas. William Perry, former executive director of the Quality Assurance Institute, said, "If quality is not improving, it's deteriorating." Quality management is a long-term, never-ending process.

Prevention orientation
Eliminate inspection and substitute prevention. By eliminating problematic root causes, prevention lowers costs by avoiding rework, unsatisfied customers, recalls and defective products and services.

Team approach
Everyone, including suppliers, management, workers and customers become equal partners in the improvement process.

Process management
Follow a structured problem-solving approach versus typical knee-jerk decision-making.

Employee empowerment
Quality management requires a unified effort from everyone in the organization. Productivity comes through harnessing the ideas and energy of all people at all levels. Management provides the resources, training and support to get the job done.

In summary, Deming's message to Japan and this country was "that they—management—were the problem, and nothing would get better until they took personal responsibility for change." His message still rings true today.

48

Dr. Deming's
14 Points for Management

1. Create constancy of purpose toward improvement of product or service. By being innovative, continuously improving everything and providing the right equipment, businesses become competitive, stay in business and provide more jobs.

2. Adopt the new philosophy. We are in a new economic age where Western management must awaken to the challenge, must learn its responsibilities, and take on a new attitude for change.

3. Cease dependence on inspection to achieve quality. Eliminate the need for inspection on a mass basis by building and designing quality into the product at the very beginning.

4. End the practice of awarding business based on price tag alone. Move toward single suppliers for any one item. Build long-term relationships with suppliers based on loyalty and trust.

5. Improve constantly and forever the system of production and service. No longer be satisfied with just "good

enough." All aspects of the business must improve constantly. By improving quality, costs decrease and morale and customer satisfaction increase.

6. Institute training on the job. Training enhances job performance. All workers and managers should receive training on the job.

7. Institute leadership. Leadership is the job of management. The aim of management is to help people and machines do a better job with less effort.

8. Drive out fear so everyone may work effectively for the organization. Management must create a secure environment and build pride of workmanship.

9. Break down barriers between staff areas. People must work together as teams. Eliminate invisible barriers between departments that cause delays and frustration.

10. Eliminate slogans, exhortations and targets for the workforce. Slogans and posters do not motivate or improve productivity. Management must seek the root causes to the problems that inhibit worker productivity.

11a. Eliminate work standards (quotas). Substitute leadership.

11b. Eliminate management by objective. Eliminate management by numbers and numerical goals. Substitute leadership.

12a. Remove barriers that rob hourly workers of their right to pride in workmanship. Management must be involved in the day-to-day struggles workers face. Most managers are too detached to what really is happening on the job.

12b. Remove barriers that rob people in management and staff of their right to pride in workmanship. Management should abolish the annual merit rating system and management by objectives. The majority of all formal evaluation systems are unfair and invalid.

13. Institute a vigorous program of education and self-improvement.

14. Put everyone to work to accomplish the transformation. Transformation is everyone's job.

This information was excerpted from OUT OF THE CRISIS, copyright 1986 by the W. Edwards Deming Institute.

49

Maintaining Ethical Leadership

William F. James said, "There are only three things necessary for success: first, normal intelligence; second, determination; and third, absolute honesty. One cannot be a little dishonest—it's all the way or nothing."

My company was brought in to work with an organization because of high employee turnover and low morale. The CEO appeared to be friendly, likeable and approachable. However, as time went by, we discovered some unethical issues that appeared to be the root cause of the negative issues we were brought in to solve.

He was manipulating employees in the accounting department so he could get a larger bonus. He used corporate funds to fly his various girlfriends to meetings, and the list went on.

When we confronted him with these issues, he showed no guilt or remorse. He no longer could tell the difference between right or wrong. The next step was to report this issue to his board of directors. They terminated his employment, but unfortunately the damage he caused created an irreparable blemish on the organization he was supposed to be leading.

Fortunately, most organizations are led by moral and ethical leaders. It saddens me to see a few misguided people bring damage to the reputation and livelihood of employees and other stakeholders. Is it unreasonable to expect those in charge to be held to a higher standard?

My point is clear and simple: Leaders have a higher standard to uphold. Whether you call yourself CEO, president, leader, manager, elected official, religious leader or supervisor, we are expected to set the example for others. The needs of those we lead should come before OUR needs. Leadership is a 24-hour-a-day responsibility.

We should not have to depend on Congress or the legal profession to tell us how to behave. You cannot legislate honesty, integrity or morality. The decision to be ethical comes from the inside—one's moral compass. Discipline from within, not from without. When deciding whether or not your actions are ethical, here are a few guidelines to consider:

- Does your personal conduct set an example for others to follow? Whether you like it or not, your personal conduct reflects your ability to lead others. Ask: would my conduct cause embarrassment to me, to my family or to my organization if it were broadcast on the 6 o'clock news?

- Is it the truth? The Cadet Honor Code at the U.S. Military Academy at West Point states, "I will not lie, cheat or steal, nor tolerate those who do." Many times it is the "toleration" that gets us in trouble. We become guilty by association when we ignore what others are doing.

- What is your personal motivation? Are you motivated by personal gain, greed or selfishness? Or are you doing your job for the common good—what is best for the organization and for individuals? If in doubt, get a group of people and ask their opinion.

- Does it violate your personal convictions? When asked to do something or faced with a choice, does it make you feel guilty?

- Does it uphold the public trust? As an official of an organization, if this action became public knowledge, would you feel proud or would it result in damage to the organization you represent?

- Do you and/or your organization deliver on its promises? Do you keep your word? In bygone days, a man's word meant everything. But today, the greed for profit sometimes gets in the way of truth in advertising. Are your organization's promises to deliver on your products and services exaggerated?

50
Managing the 20-Something Workforce

Many people carry stereotypes and perceptions about this generation. It is important to note that there are many more similarities between the generations than there are differences.

I hired a 22-year old summer intern to work for my management consulting business a few years ago. Gundrune was a recent college graduate possessing a voracious appetite to learn. She grew up in East Berlin, Germany, before the fall of the Berlin Wall. She spent two years at a university in England and this was her first trip to the United States. She spoke perfect English and in her spare time she studied Spanish. Her work ethic was unmatchable and she quickly mastered all we had to offer her. For most of her assignments, I gave her only general guidance and she effortlessly transformed her assignments into a finished project above comparison. As with most people her age, her computer skills were second to none.

The biggest difference between the younger generation and my generation is loyalty. In my day, we were loyal to the organization, no matter what. Today, members of this generation are loyal to themselves. They take personal responsibility for their own development and will dedicate themselves to the organization only if they receive dedication in return. And that is the way it should be.

51

The Importance of Having a Good Mentor

A mentor is someone who serves as a counselor or guide. Being asked to serve as a mentor is an honor. It indicates the company has faith in the person's abilities and trusts him to have a positive impact on the career and development of another person.

Many companies have discovered mentoring for new employees not only helps them settle into their jobs and the company's environment, but it also increases employee retention. The use of a mentor may be an informal, short-term situation or a more formal, long-term assignment.

In an informal mentoring program, the mentor helps the new employee for a limited period of time. The mentor may include basic work advice and information about everyday routines not found in the employee manual. A mentor can be available to answer questions, which saves time for the supervisor or manager. Furthermore, new employees often feel more comfortable asking questions of a mentor instead of their boss.

In a program of this type, mentors often are volunteers. Forcing someone to serve as a mentor can quickly create problems. Obviously, someone with a negative attitude who might encourage a new employee to gripe and complain should not serve as a mentor.

A formal version of mentoring occurs when an organization appoints an individual with specialized knowledge and experience to serve as a mentor. This process may help a new professional the company feels has excellent potential for growth. The mentor's role usually lasts for an extended period of time and may not end until the person mentored reaches an appropriate level of development.

Whether informal or formal, both parties need to understand the parameters. These may be more important in a long-term, formal mentoring situation, but can also influence the success of short-term, informal mentoring.

The mentor's role is to teach and advise the new employee. The mentor does not interfere with the supervisor or manager's decisions. The new employee, while expected to seek the mentor's advice particularly on critical issues, is not bound to accept that advice.

Confidentiality is important. Both parties need to feel confident discussions remain between them and are not relayed to a supervisor or manager.

Certain areas may be considered off-limits. The mentor needs to outline these areas at the beginning.

Decide in advance how you will communicate. Will you have regularly scheduled meetings? Will discussion be face-to-face, over the telephone or even via e-mail? Both parties need to make their preferences known at the beginning and reach an acceptable compromise if the preferences are different.

Discuss time limits. If the mentoring period has a time limit, the mentor should state that at the beginning.

Discuss time commitments. Again, this may be more critical for the long-term, formal mentoring. The mentor must expect to give the new employee adequate time, but the newcomer should not expect excessive amounts of time. Setting a schedule at the beginning avoids irritating misunderstandings later (example: meet once a week the first month, then once a month after that).

Establish openness and respect. Both the mentor and the mentee need to be open and honest, yet respect each other. A mentor who withholds important information or comments does not contribute to the other person's success. However, such comments should be delivered with tact and courtesy, and—even if somewhat hurtful—received with an open mind.

Maintain a professional relationship. The relationship between the mentor and his or her protégé is a professional one not a personal one. This is particularly important for the new employee to understand.

Ensure compatibility. It would be helpful to use a behavioral survey on both the mentee and the mentor. This will help them understand each other's communication styles, strengths, and limitations.

52

Creating Jobs with Meaning and Purpose

Do you want to find a job or do you want to have a job that gives you a sense of purpose? One core truth supersedes all backgrounds, cultures and generations: people want to be part of an organization that makes them feel important and is working for a higher cause.

When an organization means something, people are willing to give more. Let's face it, most employees have a "here today, gone tomorrow" attitude toward their work. They know their jobs may vanish when the company hits hard times or changes direction. With this kind of skeptical attitude, their loyalty to their employer may only be skin deep.

But when meaning is present, loyalty is deeper. That's why people work for nonprofit organizations or dedicate themselves to building houses for Habitat for Humanity. And it's the reason why an employer who can create meaning and purpose—and align its employees with its mission—will have a more dedicated, productive and profitable crew.

Embree Robinson is the founder and president of TRC Staffing Services Inc., a $200 million temporary staffing agency with 75 offices in the Southeastern United States and on the West Coast.

Robinson's personal experience shows there is no one way to attract, keep and motivate his hard-won workforce. According to him, many things have changed in today's workforce, but one thing remains constant: "The company must stand for something and the leadership is what makes it work."

Robinson takes this challenge personally. He stays in touch with his people as much as possible without being a micromanager. He practices a people-centered approach to management and visits about 25 branch offices a quarter. During each visit he sits down with the branch managers, listens while they discuss their goals, reviews their overall performance and tells everyone where they are heading. During the holiday season, He adds levity by giving out turkeys and Christmas presents while dressed as Santa Claus.

Robinson says people want two things out of their professional relationship: challenge and security. Challenge means the opportunity to grow professionally as well as financially. Branch managers have the option to buy into the company and become shareholders. The corporate office also rewards each branch office with a hefty 20 percent of the profits. Ten percent goes to the office managers and the other 10 percent is split among branch employees.

To feel secure, people need to know company rules and expectations. They also want their boss to keep them informed about where the company is heading. "Workers today want to know the strategic direction of the company," Robinson says. "They have ideas and expect upper management to listen to them or they will walk to the next employer who will listen and provide them the information they need and expect."

Prescription for Action

■ Ensure employees understand the mission, values and purpose of the organization.

■ Allow employees easy ability to switch jobs within the organization.

■ Conduct a comprehensive orientation program for all employees.

■ Take more time selecting employees. High retention begins with hiring the right people.

■ When hiring people, don't misrepresent the job opportunities available at your organization.

■ Allow employees opportunities to participate in volunteer activities outside work.

■ Ensure senior leaders verbalize and demonstrate organizational goals and direction.

■ Develop goals in alignment with the strategic plan.

■ Identify trends and issues that will impact on the organization.

53

Managing Personality Conflicts and Negative Attitudes

They're here, there, everywhere. They upset managers and fellow employees—even themselves. Who are "they?" If you haven't already guessed, "they" are the negative employees most people encounter in the workplace at some point. If not carefully managed, they can suck the energy out of your business and your personal life.

What is a negative employee? They are people with poisonous attitudes and behavior patterns who negatively influence the people around them. Negative workers come in various shapes and sizes. Sometimes they spread rumors, gossip about co-workers or bad mouth their superiors to their faces and behind their backs. Basically, they are unhappy people who resist the positive efforts of others.

Managers often hesitate to terminate them if they are productive or have special skills or experience. Sometimes, however, managers do not understand the amount of stress a negative employee creates. It may be hard to accept that a negative employee who did a good job did so at the expense and productivity of others. Yet, ignoring or tolerating the problems and the atmosphere they create can easily and quickly result in dissatisfaction among other employees.

What can a supervisor or manager do when faced with this unpleasant dilemma?

First, analyze the situation. How much does the person contribute to the overall success of the office, department or business? How much does he contribute to creating personality conflicts with other employees? How does that unhappiness translate into reduced productivity and enthusiasm? How much time as a manager are you using to control the situation? What are the legal ramifications (if any) of discharging the employee?

Second, plan a course of action. If you decide to try to salvage the employee, consider these tips:

■ Discuss the situation with the employee. They will probably profess ignorance of any problems, acknowledge the situation but blame the problems on others, or become defiant and try to play mind games with you. The employee may also voice his own complaints.

■ Evaluate the employee's position. Even a person with a negative attitude can have a legitimate complaint. Evaluate not only the employee's response to your remarks but whether the employee has legitimate concerns you need to consider. If the complaint is the basis of the person's negative attitude or behavior, resolving it should result in a more positive situation. Often, however, the complaint is either a smoke screen for the employee's behavior or has resulted from the person's own negativity.

- Focus on a behavior you want changed, not an attitude. Accept the reality you may not be able to remake the person into an ideal employee, even if you are a great manager. However, you can specify an action or goal for the employee, and then follow through on the employee's progress. Once you see improvement, focus on another area. Always, of course, acknowledge the employee's efforts.

- Use personality profiles and assessments. Many times, personality conflicts are the result of misunderstandings that build up over time. Each individual has a different personality style and frequently, different personality styles clash with others. A team-building session can help co-workers understand and appreciate each other in a new way. Packaged along with a personality profile or an individual behavior assessment, it can be a powerful tool in reducing conflict and improving communication between workers.

- Consider assignments that will isolate the person from other employees and limit contact. Most work situations require cooperation and teamwork that make this technique unworkable, but it may be feasible in some cases. You may even encounter an employee who prefers isolation and is less negative when working alone. Unfortunately, negative employees often seek out fellow workers—either to complain about their job, boss or life, or to blame other employees as the source of their unhappiness.

- Set a limit and stick with it. Managers have adopted the "three strikes and you're out" rule. Make the employee aware of the limits, tell them when they "strike" and remind them when they have only one "strike" left.

Third, terminate the employee. If all else fails and the negative employee ignores your warnings and refuses to cooperate, it is time to consider termination. Once you decide this is the proper course, take action. Otherwise, you risk losing the respect and confidence from your other employees. Before termination, discuss the situation with a human resources professional and seek legal counsel accordingly.

54

Seven Steps for Effective Meeting Management

Let's declare war on meetings—time wasting, poorly run, unnecessary meetings none of us feel should be required as part of our work lives. Some of us have even left the world of corporate bureaucracy to escape the endless schedule of meetings that seem longer than necessary and accomplish less than intended. But meetings cannot and should not be completely eliminated even in a small company, so let's talk about how to spend the time and effort wisely.

I attended a worldwide conference of nearly 1,000 people brought together to review and revise the policies and procedures of the organization. A committee of 1,000 can barely agree on anything and each word and sentence was intensely debated. At the end of a 10-day period, the participants were exhausted and hardly knew what they were voting on next. They just wanted to get through and go home. Every delegate had a chance to be heard, but the quality of the effort had noticeably deteriorated by the end of the conference.

First, all meetings need to have a goal or objective. It sounds elementary, but if you can't think of a desired outcome for the meeting, then why meet at all? There are plenty of good reasons to meet, including communicating information, solving problems or learning a new skill. But if you cannot easily identify one or more of these reasons, don't move past this stage of planning. Writing down the goals will help clarify and evaluate them.

Assuming you can pass the goals and objectives test, the next question is who should attend? Invite only those persons who are directly affected and/or who have relevant information. How often have you sat in a meeting wondering why you are there? It is interesting to note productivity of the group increases as new members are added but at some point, an optimal level of effectiveness is reached. If we add participants beyond this optimal point, productivity starts to decline. Fewer participants are better as the point of diminishing returns is reached quickly.

Once the goals are set and the participants determined, a few ground rules are useful:

1. Prepare a written agenda. Even if there is only one item on the agenda or the meeting is regularly scheduled, write it down and give copies to the participants. You owe it to them.

2. Arrive early. See that the meeting room is clean and necessary materials are available. Usually, something needs to be done to get a meeting place ready.

3. Start on time, end on time. It's not fair to those who arrive on time to wait for those who don't. Pace the meeting and

keep the commitment to the promised adjournment time. Participants have planned other work around it.

4. Prohibit interruptions. Don't allow outside interruptions or participants to interrupt each other. If they are present, their opinions are important.

5. Be a good participant. If you are a participant, you deserve a well-organized and a well-run meeting. Don't tolerate a poor meeting. You are also expected to contribute to the success of the meeting.

6. Be a good facilitator. If you are the meeting facilitator, state the goals and objectives, keep it on schedule and involve everyone in the process.

7. Summarize and follow up. Always review the results and develop a follow up plan to ensure agreed-upon action is taken.

Be particularly careful of establishing a standing committee that meets regularly. Attending such meetings gets to be a habit, and habits are hard to break. These meetings can become part of the company culture, and it can be politically difficult to question such an established meeting. But it takes some courage to fight the war on meetings, and don't be afraid to disband an obsolete practice.

One weapon in the fight against nonproductive meetings may be mini-meetings. It may be possible to have several informal, short meetings during the day and get more done than in scheduled and more formal meetings.

55

Strategies for an Effective Employee Orientation Program

Remember your first day on the job? Was it a good experience? Many organizations treat new hires poorly or even worse, like they have a contagious disease. Consider the first impression new people receive about your place of business.

In one organization plagued with high turnover, half the employees quit during their first week on the job. Everyone just scratched his head and hid behind the excuse, "Kids today just don't have a work ethic." Not until we sat down and started asking "why" did the real problems emerge. It was not the work ethic of the new employees, but what they were required to do their first week on the job.

As part of their orientation program, employees were required to watch 15 training videos. Many times a new employee was in the conference room by himself. The information was boring, technical and outdated. New employees were isolated the entire first day. Therefore, their first impression of this company was negative. No one took them out to lunch. No wonder that at the end of the week, they opted not to return.

Employee retention begins the first day on the job. On the larger scale, the first week on the job will determine if a new employee stays or quits 90 days from now. The first week at work should stand out in the memory of the new hire as a positive event—a celebration that makes him proud to have chosen this organization. Consider these alternatives.

Club 1230

The Boys & Girls Clubs of America has a unique way of improving retention in its Atlanta office. Once a week, leaders gather to meet and greet new employees and share news of the good things happening in the organization. This helps tear down silos, improves communication and makes everyone feel part of the same team.

Lunch Bunch

In addition to Club 1230, a department takes responsibility for the "lunch bunch." The job of the department members is to travel around the office inviting new employees to eat lunch with them. This is an excellent way to build loyalty and team spirit. Each month a new department rotates as the "lunch bunch."

It is important to build relationships and connections with co-workers during those impressionable first few days on the job. There are steps to take to ensure the first few days at work are successful and to eliminate resignations caused by unintentionally thoughtless behavior.

Before the first day:

- Mail the new employee a welcome packet. This may include logistics about the first day, an agenda of activities, directions and a congratulatory letter.

- Send them a box of, "company goodies," such as memo pads, a T-shirt, coffee mug and company logo items.

- Order their business cards far enough in advance that they are ready the day they arrive.

- Notify their team that a new person is coming, his name and role within the organization.

- Prepare the work area. Make sure it's clean and stocked with office supplies.

- Plan to have the computer, e-mail information, telephone and voice mail information ready in advance.

- Pass around a congratulations card to the new employee's team so it's signed by everyone and on his desk.

- Send a lunch invitation for the first day.

- These activities say, "We are excited you're here and we are prepared for you."

- So the day has arrived. Let's look at ideas to make the first day a stellar experience.

- First day on the job:

- Some organizations utilize the company intranet where the new employee can complete information online. This streamlines the first day so there isn't a mountain of paperwork.

- Have a "Welcome!" banner in the work area.

- Introduce the new employee to his co-workers, staff and other key personnel.

- Assign him a professional partner who will be his "buddy" within the department to get him up to speed and share "secrets" for success in the department.

- Plan an hour of uninterrupted time with the new employee's manager on the first day.

- Take him on a tour of the department. You may want to do a complete building tour a couple days later. Just let him familiarize himself with the key areas at the beginning.

- Provide a schedule or agenda if you haven't already done so.

- Assist the employee in getting his identification, security pass, codes and keys.

- Have a nameplate on his desk or at his cubicle.

- Have two new friends take him to the Human Resources department so appropriate signatures and benefits information can be completed.

- Provide a list of commonly used jargon so he understands what's being said or he can look it up.

- Give him an envelope of "Dumb Question Coupons" he can give to other people to relieve the fear of asking too many questions.

- Have a special food treat delivered to the new person.

- Provide a document of frequently asked questions from previous new employees.

- Send him home with a gift certificate to take his spouse out to dinner so they can talk about the day and relax.

- Provide a snapshot memo of what activities to expect in the next week.

56
Case Study: SAS Institute

SAS Institute Inc. is the largest, privately held software company in the United States. They are located in North Carolina's Research Triangle Park.

SAS resembles a college campus more than a software development company. Everything from the baby grand piano in the company cafeteria to the giant outdoor chess board and the resident artists give clear indication this company is a world apart. They have made Fortune Magazine's "Top 100 Best Places to Work," for several years running.

Many people say working at SAS is like working with your family. Their more than 5,000 employees find a nurturing environment and in some cases it is the closest thing to a real family that many people have experienced.

Turnover hovers around 3.7 percent and has rarely exceeded 5 percent in over two decades of existence. The average turnover rate for most industries is 15 to 30 percent. Company loyalty, which has been destroyed by many corporations, is alive and well at SAS. During the height of the dot-com boom, one SAS graphics designer turned down job offers from Silicon Valley for as much as 40 percent more money because of the work environment SAS provides. Here are some of the perks and benefits employees enjoy:

Unlimited sick leave: There is no limit on how much sick leave employees can use. Bob Goodnight, president of SAS, a Ph.D. and billionaire, believes if you treat adults like adults they will act like adults. Whether you are out sick for six days or six months, it is not a problem.

On-site day care: Employees can place their children in the on-site day care facility. Parents are encouraged to eat lunch and dinner with their children. The company cafeteria is equipped with highchairs.

Free family health care: In lieu of health insurance, SAS staffs a medical clinic 24 hours a day for employees and their family members. This saves the company hundreds of thousands of dollars a year in health insurance costs and saves thousands of hours of lost time.

Equal pay for equal work: Many businesses run off good employees because new hires are able to start making higher salaries than the "old" employees. Not at SAS. If SAS has to hire new employees and pay them more, all employees with the same skill levels receive the same pay raise.

35-hour workweeks: All employees work five seven-hour workdays. They are encouraged not to stay past 5 p.m.

Break areas and free food: Each floor has its own break area stocked with complimentary refreshments, including all the M&Ms employees can eat.

Benefits and perks can't buy loyalty, but SAS appears to have created a workplace where employees know they are cared for, trusted and treated like adults.

57
The Spaghetti Management Syndrome

Just because a person shows potential or has a degree does not mean he will be good at managing others. Many are skilled technicians but unfortunately are clueless on the art and science of managing people.

Some businesses practice what I call the "Spaghetti Management Syndrome." They pick a bunch of people, promote them to managers, then throw them on a wall like spaghetti and see what sticks. This is not the fault of the manager, but the employer. Without training and support most new managers will fail. This is one of the main reasons people today run like the plague to avoid becoming supervisors and managers.

Sure, some managers are tyrants and no amount of training is going to change them. But at least good businesses recognize their mistakes and provide additional training or find the errant manager a job somewhere else.

Good businesses place people skills as a vital part of their performance management system. For example, Synovus

Financial Corporation has been listed in the "Top 100 Best Places to Work" for several years. They have a commandment that says, "A manager's most important role is to serve, grow and inspire his or her people—with no exception." This requirement had a positive impact on the bottom line. Not only did its employee turnover rate drop, but also its market capitalization grew from $2.2 billion to $8 billion in four years.

VI

Turn Over a New Leaf—
Avoid High Turnover

58

The Workforce Skills Shortage

We do not have enough people equipped with the right skills to fill all the jobs becoming available, and it's going to get worse—a lot worse very soon. Many of these shortages are found in the skilled trades such as heavy equipment mechanics, construction workers, truck drivers, healthcare professionals and certain jobs in the IT sector to name a few.

The growth rate of the workforce has been steadily declining since the 1970s. Both the U.S. Census Bureau and a report from Accenture Consulting indicate the workforce will begin to experience a negative growth rate beginning in 2015.

The beginning of IT shortages is also starting to emerge. Google announced it was unable to meet its growth expectations because it could not find enough qualified technicians. As the economy rebounds, many more shortages will develop.

The United States has always been a beacon for skilled talent coming here from overseas. Over the past years, however, fewer people have requested educational visas, and in turn international student enrollments are decreasing. Part of this is related to September 11, 2001, but more significantly, other international cities are becoming more economically vibrant and are attracting top talent away from the U.S. For example, New Zealand, which only has a population of approximately 4 million people, now provides a home to over 40,000 Americans.

The 45 to 65 age group is the fastest growing demographic. Estimates indicate by 2020 one out of every two people in the U.S. will be older than 50. These older workers are willing to stay in the workforce longer or even re-enter it after retirement. Yet most businesses continue to cater to rapidly diminishing younger workers. A survey conducted by the Society of Human Resource Managers (SHRM) shows 65 percent of companies surveyed exerted no effort to recruit older workers for open positions. Eighty-one percent did not have benefit plans designed with older workers in mind.

As the economy grows, employee turnover will rise significantly. Research my company has conducted shows a large portion of the workforce is getting ready to "abandon ship" as the economy improves. Employees are looking for better benefits, career advancement and greater job satisfaction.

59

Job Satisfaction Survey Points to Major Workplace Issues

Chart Your Course International completed the annual Job Satisfaction Survey in July 2009. The survey focused on how people felt about their jobs and their working environment during the economic downturn. Respondents were asked 13 questions related to job frustration, trust, motivation, employee retention and communication in the workplace. Over 200 people responded to the online survey.

Several key issues were identified. The most notable change from previous surveys was how people fell about their senior executives. Over 20 percent of the respondents indicated they do not trust their executives. Additionally, more than 35 percent fell their executives do not make sound and informed decisions.

During the past 12 months, 39 percent of the workforce felt their productivity had improved on the job, while 28 percent felt it had decreased. On a positive note, 68 percent of the workforce felt motivated to do a good job. However, the majority of respondents said "poor communication" and a feeling of a "lack of appreciation" plagued most workplaces.

One question asked participants to reveal if they were going to quit or stay with their employer when the economy improves. The survey showed 49 percent of the current workforce plan on staying while 21 percent said they are definitely planning to leave. However, 29 percent indicated "they did not know."

The percentage of workers who said "they did not know" should concern employers the most. Individual comments from the survey show some businesses have resorted to a caustic, "you should be thankful you have a job" mentality. The result could have unintended consequences and could negatively impact on employers when the economy starts to rebound. Employers may face a significant percentage of workers who may abandon ship for a better place to work just when they need to ramp up. The additional recruitment, turnover and training costs could place employers in even greater financial jeopardy. A good place to work is a good place to work during good times and bad.

60

The Cost of Employee Turnover Is High

The cost of attracting, recruiting, hiring, training and getting new people up to speed is tremendously higher, as well as more wasteful, than many realize. This equates to allowing your house to burn down when you could have purchased an inexpensive smoke detector. Prevention is always less expensive and a wiser use of your resources.

Labor costs are the most expensive aspect of running a business. Even though all businesses measure profit and loss, they rarely consider how much turnover is actually costing them. Consider the annual turnover costs of a typical healthcare system ranges from $14 million to $27 million per year, according to Unifi Network, a subsidiary of PricewaterhouseCoopers LLP.

Second, productivity is directly tied to retention. Companies with high turnover are at risk for low productivity. Studies from the Gallup organization show employees who have an above-average attitude toward their work will generate 38 percent higher customer satisfaction scores, 22 percent higher productivity and 27 percent higher profits for their companies.

In spite of the staggering cost of turnover, the majority of most businesses do not have a formal retention program. Employers must focus on creating an environment that lets people work productively and effectively and makes them feel good enough to stay. Consider the following:

- Improve workforce participation rates by providing the environment and benefits attractive to an older workforce.

- Train managers on what leads to higher retention and greater job satisfaction.

- Hold managers responsible for employee retention in their departments.

- Start measuring the cost of turnover.

- Place extra effort on retaining the key individuals and key jobs that have the most impact on profitability and productivity.

- Show people the big picture. Help them understand how their job individually impacts on the overall company mission.

- Promote managers whose behavior is consistent with the organization's values and philosophies.

- Terminate or reassign managers/supervisors whose behavior is inconsistent with the organization's vision and values.

61
Achieve Results by Taking Control of Your Time

Louis Boone, a poet and novelist, once said, "I am definitely going to take a course on time management ... just as soon as I can work it into my schedule."

The most important skills I have learned in life were not taught in school. Time management is a critical leadership skill needed in today's 24/7 worklife. A person who can't manage time hurts teamwork. Poor time management makes for a poor salesperson. A teenager who doesn't show up for work on time will get fired. Best of all, managing time well reduces stress and anxiety. Included here are a few time management tips I've picked up over the years.

Know what is important.
Clearly define the most important aspects of your job—the effort that generate key results. If you don't know what that is, ask questions such as, "What has the greatest impact or value on my staff members or clients?" "What will increase sales?" Focus on the 20 percent that generates 80 percent of the results.

Prioritize and make "to-do" lists.

Now that you know what is important about your job, make a weekly to-do list. Write an "A, B or C" next to each item based on importance. At the beginning of each day, make a daily to-do list. Stop and think. Which item must be completed today? This does not include items you'd like to get done today, but only the item or items that have to be completed today.

Avoid the "feel like its."

Poor time managers base their actions on their feelings and moods. You know the type, "I know my car is on fire, but I just don't feel like calling 911 right now." Effective time management is more about habits than feelings. Most people do the easy and simple elements of their job first, like reading their e-mail, scanning the newspaper or cleaning off their desk. Good time managers do what is important first, regardless of what they feel like doing. As Nike says, "Just Do It!"

Schedule your most important project for your peak energy period.

It took me many years to figure out not everyone is a morning person like me. I hop out of bed before the sun comes up ready to head off to the office, while others don't hit their stride until 3 p.m. Therefore, during your peak energy period focus your mental and physical resources on the largest projects.

Learn to delegate.

A person who refuses to delegate will be very busy, frustrated and headed for burnout. It is not necessary for a manager to personally handle every item. One very successful regional sales manager readily attributed his success to the fact he trusted his administrative assistant to handle routine items that did not require his personal attention. This left him free to concentrate on working with sales personnel outside the office.

Toss it or file it.
Follow the rule to touch paper only once. Know what is important and throw away every piece of paper you don't think you will need. If you want to keep it, spend 10 seconds filing that important paper now rather than 30 minutes searching for it later.

Be realistic and stay flexible.
One way to create stress is to plan an unrealistic amount of work. Use common sense to recognize when you have over-scheduled yourself.

Schedule time for you.
Schedule a "personal time" appointment on your calendar each day. If someone wants to see you at that time, just say, "I'm sorry, I have an appointment." Whether you use this for personal reflection, a few quiet minutes to catch your breath or simply time to think, it's a legitimate use of time. And you will still get as much, if not more, accomplished.

Make sure your electronic planner does not cost you time.
People who use electronics enjoy the orderly convenience of a digital assistant, but sometimes it takes longer to enter and

maintain information in a gadget than to jot it down with a pencil in an old-fashioned paper planner.

Manage e-mail effectively.

The same rule applies to e-mail as to paper. Read it once and do something with it. Don't read it and then let it pile up in your inbox thinking you will get back to it. Keep your inbox clutter free. Create a "keeper" folder and transfer the mail you want to keep for later. Create another folder for "actions pending" etc. Respect other people's time and avoid forwarding those stories and jokes people love to send unless they agree to get them first. Use the delete key aggressively and delete junk e-mail without reading it. Learn to use your filters to eliminate spam.

Time is valuable, and time management can help you be more productive, successful and less stressed out so you have more time to enjoy your life.

62
Marketing and Sales Strategies to Grow Your Business

Oliver Wendell Holmes said, "The great thing in this world is not so much where we stand as in what direction we are moving." No matter what business you are in, a business-as-usual mindset will ensure your competitors are making more money than you. If you don't stand out from the competition, you may find yourself stood up by your customers. Now more than ever you have to focus, improve and possibly even change what you do to attain, retain and maintain customers.

Strategy 1: Think big
Place a mental image in your mind as if you are the largest and most successful person in your industry. How much time is consumed by routine office work someone else should be doing? Now create a plan to spend more time doing the critical tasks that will help you achieve that mental image.

Strategy 2: Be different and stand out from the competition
Jordan's Furniture sells more furniture per square foot than any other furniture store in the nation. It transformed from a family-owned business into a multimillion dollar corporation

by following a principle called "Shoppertainment." To surprise employees and customers, Barry and Eliot Tatelman dressed up like the Lone Ranger and Tonto and rode horses in their parking lot. They built an IMAX theater inside one store to entertain children while their parents shopped. When you drive around the back to pick up your furniture, they provide free hotdogs and wash your car windows.

Strategy 3: Build relationships with your customers

For each month that goes by, typically customers lose 10 percent of their buying power. Create a customer database and contact them on a regular basis. Mail them a postcard, birthday card, sales flyer or newsletter to keep your name, phone number and service on their mind. Make sure you use social media such as Twitter, LinkedIn and Facebook to keep in contact.

Strategy 4: Collect e-mail addresses

Get permission from your customers to use their e-mail address. Periodically send updates and notices to your client list. As long as you have their permission and avoid overuse, e-mail can be a powerful and inexpensive marketing tool.

Strategy 5: Hire good people

A top salesperson can outsell an average one 4-1. Successful businesses realize talent management is critical to sustaining their growth in the marketplace. Sales people must understand their strengths and have a well-defined plan to reach their potential. Many companies can provide sales assessments to identify and develop top sales people.

Strategy 6: Put a shopping cart on your web site

Online sales are still growing at a dramatic pace. This is coming from people who want to save time, avoid crowded stores, find it more convenient and appreciate the ability to shop outside of store hours. Just consider eBay for example, which generates millions of dollars of sales each year. It does not cost anything to set up an account on eBay and you pay a proportion based on the cost of the item you are trying to sell.

Strategy 7: Use pay-per-click advertising

Many business owners are finding classified advertising is not an effective use of their marketing dollars. Others find pay-per-click advertising is an easier and cheaper way to reach a larger market. Pay-per-click will ensure you receive top visibility on Web sites driving more customers to your door. Advertisers bid on keywords and the more popular the keyword, the more expensive each click is. Prices vary depending on the popularity of the word. The most popular pay-per-click advertisers are Google, Business.com, and Yahoo!

63

How to Hire Exceptional People Each And Every Time

Have you ever made a bad hiring decision? Did the person you hired turn into someone different than how he presented himself during the interview? A properly designed interviewing and hiring process could have prevented the mistake and saved you time, frustration and money.

An effective job interview is more than just asking a person a series of unrelated questions. A good process allows you to understand the applicant's behavior, values, expectations and qualifications.

The primary goal of the job interview is to determine a match between the individual and the job. Additionally, you must determine if your organization is right for the applicant. By following this process it will ensure you retain the person as long as possible and make him as productive as he can be.

Use the following guidelines to insure you hire the right person each and every time.

Step 1: Understand your purpose.

Not only are you trying to determine the best applicant for the job, but also to convince the applicant this is the best place for him to work. Sure, people want jobs, but you don't want someone to leave your company 60 days from now because your place of business was not right for him. Today's workers have choices and many job opportunities to choose from.

Step 2: Prepare in advance.

Prior to the interview make sure you understand the key elements of the job. Develop a simple outline that covers general job duties. Possibly work with the incumbent to get a better idea of what the job is about. Screen the resumes and applications to gain information for the interview. Standardize and prepare the questions you will ask the applicant.

Step 3: Outline the talents and competencies needed for the job.

Each job can have anywhere from six to 14 job competencies. Identify the behaviors, knowledge, motivations and qualities candidates need to have to be successful in the job. If the job requires special skills or a license, be sure to include it on your list. Several assessments and profiles are available to help ensure you have a good match between the applicant and the job.

Step 4: Conduct the interview.

The best interview follows a structured process. This doesn't mean the entire process is inflexible without spontaneity. Ask each applicant the same questions and score them with a consistent rating process. A structured approach helps avoid bias and gives all applicants equal footing and a fair chance. The best ways to accomplish this is by using behavioral-based questions, situational questions and role-plays.

Behavioral-based questions

- Behavioral-based interview questions are used to evaluate the applicant's past behavior, experience and judgment. Here are a few questions to consider:

- Give me an example when you ...

- Describe an incident where you went above and beyond the call of duty ...

- Tell me about the time you reached out for additional responsibility ...

- Tell me about the largest project you worked on ...

- Tell me about the last time you broke the rules ...

Situational-based questions

- Situational-based questions evaluate the applicant's judgment ability, ethics and values. The interviewer first gives the applicant a hypothetical situation such as:

- You are a manager and one of your employees has just told you he thinks another worker is stealing merchandise from the store. What should you do?

- What additional information should you obtain?

- How many options do you have?

- Should you report this to your supervisor? When?

Role-plays

- Role-plays allow applicants to demonstrate their communication skills, knowledge and ability to handle stressful situations. For example, if you interview a customer service representative, you can use a role-play to see how this person can manage an irate customer. When using a role-play, consider the following guidelines.

- It is a good idea to write the situation down on paper. Give the person time or a short break to "get into character" prior to beginning the role-play.

- Give the candidate clear guidelines and background information so he thoroughly understands the situation.

- Allow him to ask questions before you begin.

- Debrief the applicant at the conclusion of the role-play. Ask him to tell you how he thought he did and how he could have done it differently.

- Conclude the role-play and provide positive feedback to the candidate. Keep in mind the stress of the job interview can influence how the person performs during the role play.

64

Use Assessments to Develop People for Professional and Personal Growth

You have worked hard to hire and train a good management team. George has worked with you for three months. His communication style is direct. He has many innovative ideas and is good at starting projects, but weak on finishing what he starts. Mary, on the other hand, is good at details. She finishes what she starts, but seems to lack initiative. Jose is a great team builder and keeps the team motivated. His only weakness is time management. He has to be reminded to finish his projects on time. Victoria is bright and intelligent, but lacks social skills. She prefers to stay in her office and send e-mail messages to her co-workers. You ask yourself, "Why can't everyone just be like me?"

In my younger days, I had a narrow approach to managing others. I believed people who did not respond to my management style were DEFECTIVE. I evaluated everyone with the same broken yardstick. I now know I was wrong. There are eight different, but predictable, work styles or behavior patterns common in people.

Many individuals are unaware of their defective behavior patterns. Their blindness will damage their personal effectiveness. When a manager understands these unique differences he is in a more powerful position. He is better able to manage, understand and lead people toward higher levels of productivity, reduce frustration, improve teamwork and increase retention.

Behavior assessments can help:

- Individuals identify their strengths, know which jobs for which they are best suited and design a development plan to overcome shortcomings;

- Human resources managers predict a job applicant's success before he is hired;

- Business owners understand the temperament and work style of individual employees and managers;

- Supervisors give performance feedback to people in a style they understand and accept for improving performance, and accelerate professional development;

- People enhance communication and understanding, and improve personal relationships; and

- Sales managers select, hire, develop and motivate super sales people.

One company used assessments to improve its hiring and recruiting process. Previously, the company made hiring decisions based only on the candidate's resume and then hired the person based on a gut reaction. Once hired, many of these new people created friction, displayed bad work ethics and exhibited attitudes that had a negative impact on their coworkers.

By using assessments this company created a visual bench-mark (graphic) of its top performers. It used another profile to identify the values, emotional competencies and behav-iors needed for success based on the requirements needed by each department (sales, customer service, management, tech support, quality assurance, etc). As a result, the company had a roadmap for hiring top people. It identified the behavior patterns, communication styles, motivations and attitudes of its top employees. In other words, the business cloned its top performers.

Most assessments available on the market today are admin-istered over the Internet and generate an amazing amount of detail. One assessment provides over 25 pages of information including:

- Personal characteristics;
- Value to the organization;
- Checklist for communicating;
- Don'ts on communicating;
- Ideal work environment;
- Perceptions;
- Keys to motivating;
- Keys to managing;
- Areas for improvement;

- Action plan for improvement

Successful management development programs first begin with self-analysis. When you understand behavior styles, then you have a roadmap for improved potential and enhanced communication. One assessment identifies eight unique behavior patterns people fall into depicted on a wheel. The behavior styles are:

- Implementer;

- Conductor;

- Persuader;

- Promoter;

- Relater;

- Supporter;

- Coordinator; and

- Analyzer

Many times I am asked to work with groups of people who experience difficulty working together and/or meeting objectives. I worked with one organization that failed to reach its sales goals.

After completing a behavior assessment on each of the directors, the problem was clear. The executive director and two assistant directors possessed the same personality style—all three of them disliked confrontation. Their natural tendency was to go overboard to please people. They did not like to hold people accountable. After they understood their natural tendencies, they were able to adapt and manage more effectively.

Developing people is less expensive than firing them. By understanding each person's behavior differences, an organization can align an employee's motivations with the company's mission. Assessments also help individuals reduce conflict and get along better. Furthermore, co-workers appreciate each other's unique strengths and abilities. With this knowledge organizations and managers can maximize the abilities of their workforce in ways to help make all employees star performers.

Index

About the Author

Greg Smith is the founder and President of Chart Your Course International Inc. As a business strategist, he helps executives and business owners accelerate business performance and navigate through accelerated rates of change. He and his cadre of business performance specialists design strategies and processes to grow your organization and implement business initiatives, creating clearer direction, increased profitability, stronger executive teams, improved communication and happier and more productive employees.

He has addressed organizations in 26 countries. Some of his clients include Malcolm Baldrige National Quality Award winners and Fortune Magazine's "Top 100 Best Places to Work."

Prior to starting his own company, Smith built his career on the front line as a U.S. Army Officer. His career culminated as a consultant to the U.S. Army Surgeon General. As the Director of Quality Management and Strategic Planning for the U.S. Army Medical Department, he played a major role in "Reinventing the Government" efforts spearheaded by the Vice President of the United States.

Smith served on the Board of Examiners for the Malcolm Baldrige National Quality Award, the nation's highest honor for business excellence. He has received many awards and honors including being listed in Harvard University's Profiles in Business and Management: An International Directory of

Scholars and Their Research. Human Resource Executive magazine selected him as one of the nation's top 10 "Rising Stars" in Human Resource Management.

Smith has written and published over 350 articles and nine books including, *401 Proven Ways to Retain Your Best Employees, The New Leader: Bringing Creativity and Innovation to the Workplace* and *Here Today, Here Tomorrow: Transforming Your Workforce from High Turnover to High-Retention.* He has appeared on numerous television programs including Bloomberg Business News and PBS television.

Chart Your Course International Inc.
2814 Ga. Highway 212, S.W.
Conyers, GA 30094
800-821-2487
(Direct) 770-860-9464 (Fax) 770-760-0581
www.Chartcourse.com
Email: Greg@ChartCourse.com